The Power of Storytelling

The Power of Storytelling

Social Impact Entertainment

Robert Rippberger

with additional writing by
Spencer Moleda

REGENT PRESS
Berkeley, California
2022

[paperback]

ISBN 13: 978-1-58790-601-5

ISBN 10: 1-58790-601-5

[e-book]

ISBN 13: 978-1-58790-602-2

ISBN 10: 1-58790-602-3

Library of Congress Catalogue Number: 2022046146

For information contact: www.SIESociety.org

Book and Cover design by On It Service

First Edition

10 9 8 7 6 5 4 3 2 1

Manufactured in the United States

REGENT PRESS

www.regentpress.net

CONTENTS

FOREWORD

by Howard Roffman

For thirty-seven years, I had a job that allowed me to experience the power of storytelling in ways that most people never can. Day after day, I witnessed the truth that Rob Ripp-berger describes so compellingly in the book you're about to read.

My job was at Lucasfilm, the company that George Lucas established when he began his filmmaking career.

Of the countless stories that have been created and told during our lifetimes, few, if any, have been as impactful as the *Star Wars* saga. My job at Lucasfilm had me overseeing every ancillary use made of *Star Wars*—from toys to books to video games and everything in between. Together, George and I managed the entire *Star Wars* brand. George had an interesting way of describing our respective roles. We were two parts of a Trinity, he liked to say. He, as the creator of the films and TV shows, was the Father; I was the Son; and the fans were the Holy Spirit. It was the kind of playful yet insightful overstatement that George loves to make.

For all his playfulness, however, George was always thoughtful and deliberate when it came to *Star Wars* storytelling. Every aspect of the stories he told was there for a well-thought-out and usually well-researched purpose. For the original *Star Wars: A New Hope* in 1977, he studied Joseph Campbell's classic work on mythology, *The Hero With a Thousand Faces,* to help him craft a story that could use allegory to impart values and important psychological lessons to children. For The Empire Strikes Back, concerned about the impact on kids of learning that Darth Vader was Luke Skywalker's father, he consulted the esteemed psychologist Bruno Bettelheim, whose seminal work *The Uses of Enchantment* focused on the emotional and symbolic importance of fairy tales for children. For *Return of the Jedi,* he used America's experience in the Vietnam War to inform a story that told how a group that others might see as primitive and underdeveloped—the Ewoks—could in fact help to defeat the superior forces of a mighty empire.

In crafting the *Prequel Trilogy* years later, before writing a single word, George carefully laid out the themes he wanted the movies to address, such as the importance of letting go, the dangers of attachment, how democracies fall and ruthless dictatorships rise up in their place. George became a student of so many disciplines—from history to psychology to religion—in fashioning the stories that together constitute his *Star Wars* saga.

Doing my job at Lucasfilm meant becoming immersed in the ways audiences around the world connected with *Star Wars,* and what I saw confirmed the genius of George's approach. For its millions of fans, *Star Wars* was much more than a wildly entertaining series of films. It was an intricately crafted modern mythology that accomplished what the greatest mythologies of humankind have done for millennia: it became a powerful allegory that speaks to the things that matter most to us as human beings—what it means to be good or evil, the power of the choices we make, the opportunity each of us has to be a hero, the importance of spirituality, and the interconnectedness of all things. People see themselves in the hero's journey of Luke Skywalker, the farm boy who steps into a larger world and discovers his inner power, helped along the way by mentors and friends, confronting his demons and ultimately finding enlightenment. The elements of that journey have become icons of our time, touching and inspiring countless millions of people now spanning more than three generations.

I got to see that influence play out day after day during my many years at Lucasfilm. I saw how *Star Wars* brought people together and created a collective experience and a sense of community; how much joy people experienced sharing *Star Wars* with their friends and introducing *Star Wars* to their kids; the ways that the fantasies kids acted out with their *Star Wars* toys were fundamental to their development as human beings. I heard countless stories from people whose lives had been touched by *Star Wars,* whether in the career choices they made, the comfort the film gave them through trying times, the reinforcement of their belief in a higher power, or their faith in themselves.

The fact that *Star Wars* can be quantified as a business proposition measured in dollars generated, number of times seen, number of items sold, is quite secondary to the unquantifiable aspects of the franchise—the values it has taught, the enhancement of our lives it has brought about, the changes to our culture it has spawned. Imagine, if you can, a world in which Luke Skywalker and Darth Vader never existed, R2-D2 and C-3PO had never bickered, the Millennium Falcon had never made the jump to hyperspace, and Princess Leia had never said "I love you!" only to hear Han Solo reply "I know." Worse yet, a world in which no one had ever uttered the words "May the Force be with you." Unthinkable!

I realize, of course, that *Star Wars,* with all its extraordinary power, is an outlier. Few storytelling vehicles in modern times can match its reach, its success, or its impact. Still, the point remains the same. The power of storytelling is universal and regularly experienced on much smaller but no less impactful scales.

Trust me, I know.

As a gay teenager growing up in the sixties, confused about my identity in a culture where homosexuality was criminalized, concealed, and condemned, I turned to the few sources in popular culture that might help guide me. I snuck into the X-rated Midnight Cowboy, John Schlesinger's Oscar-winning film in which the young cowboy Joe Buck, newly arrived in Manhattan, is "reduced" to turning tricks for closeted gay men who grovel pathetically before him, one of whom he brutally assaults. I secretly went to see Boys in the Band, William Friedkin's film of the acclaimed Mart Crowley play, hoping that none of my friends would catch me. What I saw on screen was a group of closeted gay friends in New York camping it up at one of their apartments until an old—and straight—college buddy of the party-thrower shows up unannounced and boiling over with conflict and judgment, an encounter that ends in despair for his now-outed and miserable friend. I read Giovanni's Room, James Baldwin's classic novel from the 1950s in which David, a closeted American expat in Paris currently engaged to a young woman, falls in love with Giovanni, a bright-eyed and hopeful young Italian, but is ultimately unable to overcome his own self-hatred and deserts his lover, who becomes desperate, kills a man, and is eventually executed for murder.

Each of these works is a masterpiece crafted by brilliant gay storytellers and of unquestionable historic significance. Each spins a very different yarn but all share a common message of self-loathing and tragic fates. Highly acclaimed as they were, I would venture to guess that collectively they have been experienced by fewer than the number of people who see a *Star Wars* film on a single day of its opening weekend. That didn't blunt their impact on me. These stories told me that all the horrible things I'd heard about homosexuality growing up were true. For a lost teenager struggling to find his way in the hostile world of suburban Philadelphia, they were powerful enough to cause untold confusion and pain, and to nail the closet door shut for many years to come.

There is no storytelling that doesn't deliver a message—good, bad, or indifferent, intentional or not. The same power that can educate, inspire, and enlighten can also be a source of oppression and harm. It's long been said that the pen is mightier than the sword. Rob's book is an eloquent reminder that those who forego the sword and choose the pen assume a weighty responsibility. As wielders of the mightiest of weapons, they must always be mindful of the message, for theirs is the power to lift us up or drag us down, the power to make a difference in our lives.

— *Howard Roffman*

ACKNOWLEDGEMENTS

When writing a book built on lifetimes of inquiry and research, there are a myriad of people to thank, and I cannot possibly name them all. The basis of this work is to ask: how can we have a positive impact on the world? How can we better understand the role of stories in the maturation and transformation of our lives? And where does meaning reside amidst all of this?

First, Miguel Sabido and Sergio Alarcón have shed such strong light on all three of these questions as both philosophers and practitioners that I must acknowledge not only their work and legacy but also their friendship and generosity of time in giving feedback on the book as I inquired deep into the nature of Social Impact Entertainment and its effects.

Second, I want to thank Tobias Deml, a colleague of mine at SIE Society, Cinema of Change magazine and a great friend, who unearthed some of the content that made this book possible through his own study and the podcast interviews we conducted together.

Last but not least is Spencer Moleda, who did additional writing in the book and was vital to its creation.

As additional acknowledgment, I also want to thank editor Melissa Stein, fact-checkers Anne Healey and Monica Geraffo, Barbara Fuller of Editcetera, and those that have guided this process directly and indirectly such as Glenn Sparks, Joshua Oppenheimer, Mark Litwak, Nicholas Paige, Linda Williams, Nancy Cushing-Jones,

Chris Temple and Zach Ingrasci, Courtney Spence, Philip Zimbardo, Michael Taylor, Kathy and Amy Eldon, Michael Gene Sullivan, Jeanne Meyers, Lee Mun Wah, Bill Ryerson, Sonny Fox, Don Hahn, Roberto Mangabeira Unger, Hubert Dreyfus, Albert Bandura, my colleagues at SIE Society and the PGA's Social Impact Entertainment Task Force—William Nix, Rebecca Graham Forde, Kia Kiso, Kate McCallum, Anne Marie Gillen, Laura Herb, Hiroki Kamada, Devon Dansky, Isabella Dujarric, Frank Connelly, Ed Lantz, Susan Krenn, Jane Brown, Jeff Chao, Christina Lindstrom, Kayvan Mashayekh—and at the United Nations, Carlos Islam, Andi Gitow, Jon Herbertsson, and Jeffrey Brez.

When working in any tradition, one stands on the shoulders of greats in an attempt to get closer to the stars. Thank you to those named and those who may have been left out, who got us so far already.

INTRODUCTION

Essayist and novelist Joan Didion said it best: "We tell ourselves stories in order to live."[1] She was referring to white lies, the tiny self-deceptions that allow us to maintain hope and forward momentum. In many ways, though, her statement applies to and speaks to the whole history of storytelling.

Stories are some of humankind's most powerful creations. They teach us, open doors for self-reflection, and reassure us in times of uncertainty. They are a way of giving us reference points that can illuminate different ways of being in the world while guiding us in how to be our best selves.

Critics may dismiss some forms of storytelling, such as movies, music, or comic books, as a distraction from what's in front of us, but the reality is that they are integral: they are a necessity to our survival as a species.

And that is true of all forms of storytelling, and there are many. Not that these modes can be conflated so simply, but music is an attempt to communicate feelings and ideas too delicate for prose or comment. Paintings and photographs attempt to tell stories with a single wordless image to which we can bring our own feelings and impressions. Poems are miniature, maximally truncated stories with arcs, journeys, and messages that put the limits of human brevity on trial. Even journalism, though relaying real-world events, is as essential a form of storytelling as any other.

But just for a moment, let us strip away the form factor. Before Gutenberg invented the printing press, or even before the ancient

Greeks chiseled information on stone tablets, we still managed to find ways to create, invent, and convey. When we weren't passing down stories orally through generations like precious family heirlooms, we were using cave paintings, a few fortunate specimens of which remain, that somehow brought our words to life even as we were discovering words in the first place.

Have you studied some of those cave paintings? Really taken them in? One can almost feel the faded desperation of a creature and community trying to make sense of life the only way they knew how.

In fact, it may have been this desperation that evolved storytelling from a record of events into an exercise in coping with life's unknowns. Who am I? Where do I come from? What is my place in this vast universe, one that seems only to get bigger every day? These are the questions we had thousands of years ago, and they are the questions we have now; it has been our attempt to answer them that makes storytelling such an important backbone of civilization. The answers to these questions became Greek, Roman, and Egyptian mythologies, moral stories that explained the mechanics of our natural environment while providing lessons to nurture our interior world. The three most widespread and enduring religions—Judeo-Christianity, Islam, and Hinduism—all rely on stories and fables as the moral fabric connecting vast populations across space and time.

As science matured, so did the ambitions of the storytellers. The more specific our answers to lifelong questions became, the more specific our feelings and concerns about them became. Some human questions have only human answers, and stories allow us to make peace with them. We turn to technology for practical solutions to big problems, but often these solutions give rise to larger fears and anxieties, which are perfect for storytelling because art isn't necessarily about answers, or indeed solutions—it's about the expression of our human frustrations and wonder.

George Orwell and Philip K. Dick both used storytelling to give voice to the anxieties that were such natural products of the times in which they lived, and those anxieties still continue to this day. People connected with these works. It didn't matter that storytelling didn't offer change—it offered something just as valuable: a confirmation that like-minded people are not alone in their restlessness. As Martin Heidegger worked out in "The Origin of the Work of Art," great art crystallizes and shines for the culture all that it is thinking but cannot articulate, bringing people together to bask in its light.[2]

As we use stories to make peace with being human, we pass them down to the generations succeeding us. Storytelling becomes essential to how people are raised and mature in society and as a society. Exposure to storytelling allows children to connect with ideas they lack the years or experience to fully understand, and it inspires them to form new ideas of their own.

How many children's fairy tales have become cornerstones of our emotional and intellectual development? How many Aesop's fables have been told, retold, reworked, reimagined, and otherwise mined for their timeless power and wisdom? And how many people are taught the value of truth through the story of "The Boy Who Cried Wolf"? These tales are not simply amusing flights of fancy, though they are occasionally that as well; they are our very introduction to the rules of life. They challenge our preconceptions and place our values under scrutiny when any alternative method would be too complex for budding minds.

On a more cultural level, storytelling also informs our behavior and self-perception. The image of James Dean in Nicholas Ray's touchstone movie Rebel Without a Cause (1955) forever changed what it looked and felt like to be masculine.[3] Through examples like these, storytelling becomes a mirror in which our own values are reflected. One need only to look at the evolving roles for women and people of color in literature, television, and movies to see a timeline of society's attitudes toward these demographics, bending toward justice.

How one defines being a man, woman, adult, child, and everything in between is often sourced from the stories we were told from birth. Stories express how we determine what's brave, what's weak, what's offensive, and what's admirable. Traditionally men are strong, courageous, and noble, whereas women are sensitive and nurturing. Men are billed as heroes, and women are billed as objects of romance and power, ultimately coupled with the heroes of the stories we grew up with. These stories ossify our present values, which is why they are retold, modernized, and reinterpreted to clear the way for progress.

Since storytelling is an essential part of being human, changing with us rather than becoming obsolete, it says something profound that in a time as technologically advanced as our own, our most essential advancement remains our ability to communicate feelings and ideas and make them anew.

As long as there are questions humans can ask, we will turn to storytelling to provide answers that simply do not exist in nature and in science. And from there, it's not much of a stretch to suggest that if we change our storytelling, we can therefore change ourselves and our relation to collective existence.

Storytelling and the storytellers who breathe life into new possible worlds enrich us all in a conversation of what are our values, what is important, who am I, what is a good life, how should we relate to technology, along with countless other questions that have confounded us from the very beginning. Storytelling reflects back, but it can also write the future. According to Bill Moyers, professor and mythology scholar Joseph Campbell once told him, "If you want to change the world, change the metaphor."[4]

Chapter 1

ENTERTAINMENT-EDUCATION OR SOCIAL IMPACT ENTERTAINMENT (SIE)

If someone off the street told you that one man set out to make a series of six soap operas to raise Mexico's standard of living, and dramatically helped decrease population growth that had been exponential for more than ten years—all substantiated by scientific research—you might think it was an extended setup to an incredibly complicated practical joke.

It sounds like something plucked from an activist's fever dream of best-case scenarios—the world simply doesn't work that way, or so the more cynical would have you assume. Fade in on the world of Miguel Sabido, a man who wasn't focused on how the world worked presently. In the fashion of a true visionary, he was focused on how it could work, given a specific methodology and the right amount of tenacity. His goal was to use media for a proven social benefit.

It is not easy to define Sabido: producer, communication researcher, playwright, filmmaker, director, and activist for the rescue of traditional theater. He defines himself as a communication theoretician and practitioner obsessed with finding the social use of entertainment.[5]

In Sabido's view, it is the responsibility of storytellers to consider the ways they can shape their audiences for the betterment of society. That impassioned sense of social responsibility was not reserved to his profession; it was so deeply rooted in his Mayan heritage and childhood that to do anything else would feel out of character.[6]

Sabido's grandmother founded the first school for social workers in Mexico, and his mother worked as a volunteer teaching remote indigenous communities across the country about symbols and customs such as the Mexican national flag and national anthem.[7] Sabido's father, who grew up in one of these indigenous communities and didn't learn Spanish until he was a teenager, made Sabido aware at a very young age of the many atrocities committed in the process of Mexican colonization.[8] Being surrounded by such humanitarian ideals fertilized Sabido's compassion and sense of civic community, and as he transitioned into adulthood, he sought to deploy these ideas.

As a college student, Sabido enrolled at the National Autonomous University of Mexico, a school known for its focus on public research. He began to see that if our first and greatest human advancement was learning to communicate effectively, perhaps rekindling and focusing that ancient spark could aid many of the problems plaguing the modern world.

Although Sabido retained a firm grasp on his passions for social change after college, he was at first more acclaimed as a skilled director of actors, having cut his teeth in the theater scene in the 1950s.[9] It was during this time that he formulated what he labeled the Theory of the Tone, a system that could allow an actor to inspire emotion in the audience rather than simply convey it clinically.[10] While expanding his ideas, Sabido wondered if the same kind of emotional connection to the audience could be invoked to effect social change. It was this trajectory that led him to cross paths with Televisa, the largest mass media communications organization in the Spanish-speaking world.[11]

Sabido started his career at Televisa as general director of evaluation, overseeing the shows on the network while making proposals to strengthen engagement. His clarity of vision gave him wings in the organization. Within two months, after impressing the president with his theories, he ascended the ranks to become vice president of evaluation.

In this position, Sabido was the middleman between the department of producers and the CEO of Televisa. Their meetings were long and crowded, filled with people looking to fine-tune their programming for maximum-but-precise reach and appeal. For some, it was probably just another 8:00 a.m. obligation. Little did they know that the world was about to change—Sabido used his background in communication to develop a system that not only shaped the actor's performances but also shaped entire programs based on what audiences responded to with the most zeal.

According to Sabido's pitch, virtually all Latin American dramas follow a familiar scheme:

1. A desperate protagonist is attempting to overcome a life-limiting obstacle, whether that's poverty, following a dream, or even having children.
2. A trigger arises for three changes of fortune for the principal character, such as a crumbling marriage, suicide, a classic boy-girl meet-cute, or anything that introduces disorder into the main character's established reality.

3. A confrontation occurs between the protagonist and the antagonist, typically an overbearing mother-in-law.
4. An encounter leads to a final change of fortune, provoking a new horizon for our hero.
5. The happy ending everyone hoped for arrives, in which our character reaches their destination, internal or otherwise.

Sabido's innovation was adding extra focus to second- or third-tier plots of an otherwise mainstream telenovela with commercial appeal. These storylines would occupy no more than 20 percent of the drama so as not to distract from the more commercially friendly storylines.[12] For the slickly packaged result, Sabido coined the name "Entertainment-Education (EE)": socially conscious storylines delivered to as wide an audience as possible.

Sabido's enthusiasm for social change through entertainment was nourished by the success of the late-'60s Peruvian soap opera Simplemente María, one of the most culturally revered daytime Spanish-language programs of its era.[13] The story follows the titular character, Maria, as she sheds her suffocating village existence to try to carve a place for herself in the big city, where she cares for her son by becoming a seamstress and attending literacy courses.[14] The series wasn't simply making splashes in viewership; it also produced a noticeable spike in people buying sewing machines, particularly the brand Singer as depicted in the show.[15]

Where marketers would see spiking opportunities for product placement, Sabido had a grander, more humanistic vision: what if this kind of behavioral influence could be used not to sell Singer sewing machines but to motivate people to act on important social issues and initiatives?[16] This was among the first in-action examples of Entertainment-Education, which is referred to today also as Social Impact Entertainment (SIE).

As Sabido himself would discover, this groundbreaking idea was being mirrored in a lot of revolutionary research in psychology in the 1960s.[17] He may have been a pioneer, but thankfully, he wasn't facing his challenges without allies.

The original Entertainment-Education team included Sergio Alarcón, a spirited man fluent in English and deeply connected internationally; along with Sabido's sister Irene, who was an executive producer for television; and Carmen Galindo, an academic. They all met in 1974 at the very first annual World Encounter of Communications in Acapulco, where entertainment figures and researchers converged from France, Brazil, Portugal, Germany, Italy, and the United States to discuss various models of telecommunication across the globe.[18]

In an effort to make their focus as sharp, calculated, and impactful as possible, they enlisted the guidance of psychologist Albert Bandura, the originator of social learning theory and the theoretical construct of self-efficacy—a term used to describe a person's confidence in achieving their goals and thus continuing down a road of success rather than being discouraged and stopping.[19] Upon discovering Bandura's work, Sabido and Alarcón were so inspired that they traveled to Stanford for a face-to-face meeting.[20]

A 2002 study ranked Albert Bandura as the fourth most cited psychologist of the twentieth century, behind Jean Piaget, B. F. Skinner, and none other than Sigmund Freud.[21] Bandura began his career when television was still seen by many as an enemy rather than an educational tool.[22] He spent his early career researching the effects on developing minds of viewing onscreen violence.[23]

Bandura observed that while watching violence does not necessarily beget copycat violent behavior, exposure to violence on television does have five kinds of impact:

1. It introduces viewers to new, detailed executions of violence.
2. It affects restraint over use of violence in interpersonal relationships.
3. It tends to trivialize and normalize violent behavior through "good guys" who take advantage of violence in the name of justice.
4. It affects our emotional learning, meaning we come to like what our models like, dislike, and fear.
5. It shifts the public perception of reality.[24]

No small or insignificant effects here. And further, Bandura found that when audiences observe characters similar to themselves who get things done and persevere, they have an even stronger desire to model what these characters do—a trait he referred to as "perceived self-efficacy."

Bandura found that efficacy affects behavior in four categories:

1. Tendency toward pessimistic or optimistic thoughts
2. Development of personal aspirations, and perseverance in the face of difficulties achieving them
3. Vulnerability to emotional states such as stress, depression, and other obstacles in our emotional life

4. And most crucially, decision-making ability at critical, fight-or-flight moments[25]

In the television programs we enjoy or the movies we watch, when we see a certain character we identify with dealing with a bad breakup or a dire life-or-death circumstance, we often internalize those behaviors and motivations and replicate them in our own lives. The effect is nuanced, but this dynamic is significant in shaping our own stories.[26]

The most widely known fruition of Bandura's ideas came in the form of the trendsetting Bobo doll experiments conducted in 1961 and 1963 at Stanford. In these experiments, children were exposed to aggressive models of behavior, and through the outlet of a weighted inflatable doll, were given time and space in which to replicate that behavior if they so desired. The interest for Bandura, however, wasn't in whether or not they would inflict violence on the doll—he was interested in the complexity of the violence kids were capable of recreating based on exposure to their models. These kids wouldn't simply kick the doll out of momentary frustration—they'd hurl rocks at it, pick up tools like mallets and use them to attack, and throw the doll high in the air with aggressive charge. Most telling, though, was the fact that the only children to exhibit extreme behavior were the ones exposed to a model of it beforehand—the rest stayed perfectly, peacefully put.[27]

The Bobo doll experiment was one of the many studies that first caught Sabido's interest, as here was a leader of his academic field using hard science to cement what Sabido and his team had developed thousands of miles away in Mexico City. The next step was identifying social problems and understanding how to best address them using Entertainment-Education.

In 1975 nearly half the workforce in Mexico was illiterate.[28] The Mexican government established what should have been a very effective literacy program: people who knew how to read would create their own study groups subsidized by the government, and these groups would be given all the resources they needed in order to meet and learn on their own terms.[29] This plan was based on a very basic philosophy: give people the tools they need to educate themselves. The problem, though, was that for some reason, illiterate people were not signing up for these free services.[30] What was the barrier? What was failing to hook people?

Through a survey conducted by Sabido, it was discovered that people who could not read and were in need of these courses had a very low sense of self-efficacy, despite having the ability to learn. This is where Entertainment-Education came into play. In contrast to social programs working one-on-one to raise the efficacy of individuals, Sabido's soap operas aimed for mass influence: they created characters who went through every step of the literacy enrollment process, encouraging audiences to feel not only motivated to enroll but also fully equipped with the information to do so.

The first of these serial soaps was a drama called Ven conmigo, which broadcast between 1975 and 1976.[31] Featuring a character named Eduardo, an aging man who decided to take the very literacy courses that failed to connect with Mexican citizens, the telenovela culminated in a beautiful scene in which he read a self-written letter to his daughter for the very first time.[32]

Was that emotional punch enough to have the influence Sabido intended? Bet on it. The day after the episode aired, more than 250,000 workers stampeded to the appropriate informational hubs to secure booklets on how to follow in Eduardo's footsteps.[33] During the year after Sabido's soap first hit the air, nearly a million people enrolled in literacy classes in Mexico, a ninefold increase over the previous year.[34]

The success of Ven conmigo paved the way for perhaps Sabido's most effective use of Educational-Entertainment to date, another serial drama called Acompáñame that ran for nine months between 1977 and 1978.[35] The drama tackled the exponential and unsustainable population growth at the time in Mexico, a largely Catholic nation. The story followed a young lady in a large family in an impoverished city, trapped in an environment of crime and violence. In order to take her life into her own hands and to avoid being stranded in her circumstances forever, the protagonist decided to use contraceptives to limit the size of her family.[36]

The series was like any other soap opera—brightly lit, toned with a certain bouncy spice, colorfully costumed, and electric with all the histrionic melodrama that makes a telenovela drug-like in addictiveness. In other words, exactly as Sabido had envisioned. The audience was compelled to empathize with the protagonist's life and feel satisfied when she used the resources available to her. More than 560,000 women found their way to family planning clinics over the next year, and the increase in sales of contraception countrywide went from 7 percent the preceding year to 23 percent in the year after the series aired.[37] That's quite a rise in sales.

Though that's not all—the number of calls to Mexico's National Population Council increased 500 percent.[38] With all of these factors coming into play, plus a wealth of other similarly themed soap operas (many of them also Sabido-helmed), the period from 1977 to 1986 saw the national population growth rate plummet by 34 percent.[39] Thomas Donnelly, head of USAID in Mexico, stated that the majority of people who flocked to family planning clinics did so because they watched the telenovelas by Sabido and felt it within their efficacy to make a change.[40] Thomas Donnelly remarked,

> Throughout Mexico, wherever one travels, when people are asked where they heard about family planning, or what made them decide to practice family planning, the response is universally attributed to one of the soap operas that Televisa has done. . . . The Televisa family planning soap operas have made the single most powerful contribution to the Mexican population success story.[41]

In 1986 the United Nations awarded Mexico with its Population Award for its efforts in creating effective population control through broadcasting.[42]

Shortly in Sabido's wake, it became fashionable for producers, even those within Televisa, to try to copy the Entertainment-Education method, but none were successful because they didn't use the rigorous theoretical framework or take full advantage of the infrastructure around their viewership.

"If you do not have the infrastructure, you will fail. Do not even try my method," remarked Sabido in conversation.[43] And while this message might seem harsh, it's also easy to see his point. After all, in Sabido's mind, the only people who can change a problem are those who belong to the group impacted by that problem. It isn't enough to raise awareness if people aren't equipped to create change for themselves.

It's like Coca-Cola—you can advertise it with sweeping scope, but if you don't have the bottle in stores, people won't know where to buy it and therefore will not drink it. It's that simple. The key to

Sabido's success wasn't just his ability to connect people to the problems surrounding them but also his skill in providing instructions that allowed people to solve their problems using available government or nonprofit resources.

Another of the biggest hurdles for Entertainment-Education was conquering the lack of genuine creative talent behind the scenes. Prior to Sabido, positive impact initiatives were usually backed by educational professionals rather than entertainment professionals—their focus was so dominated by the educational perspective that there was no room for the entertainment side.[44] Sabido enlisted the skills of experienced producers, real screenwriters, and real production coordinators in order to present Entertainment-Education as entertainment first and foremost. His thinking was always that in order to work as education, it needed to work as entertainment.[45] This was the reason the EE plot usually took up no more than 20 percent of the story. That way the message didn't alienate people by permeating the full scope of the drama.[46] It was a perfect way of nourishing people with useful knowledge without it feeling procedural.

In lower-income, less privileged areas and countries, telenovelas are not just entertainment—they are a platform for communal bonding. The television is on during the day as background noise, and at night, people invite their friends over to join in and watch together. It's an event—an often-overlooked binding element in the family dynamic. And the shows over which they bond are the shows they relate to. That's the secret to Entertainment-Education—placing the information in a context viewers can personally identify with, or in terms of Bandura's theory, a positive model of behavior to learn and apply.

It's not an unusual idea. Even United States millennials and Gen Zers, who don't flock to broadcast television in the same way, are still flocking to episodic series featured on prominent subscription platforms. And how does this programming propagate? The same way: through community. Entertainment-Education is clearly able to make measurable impact, and despite remaining largely unaware of its work and theories, Hollywood has frequently attempted to launch similar initiatives.

"They're trying to reinvent the wheel when we already invented the wheel forty years ago," Sergio Alarcón remarked in an interview, going on to say, "It doesn't harm them to do the things that we did. It's better to do good instead of doing bad or doing mediocre things."[4] For Sabido, Entertainment-Education isn't simply a charity-of-the-week—it's the social responsibility of every storyteller.

Chapter 2

THE STORY OF EATING DISORDERS IN FIJI

In many ways, Western society is practically a planet on its own terms—it creates drastically different climates both literal and social, and for both better and worse, it possesses a virtually irresistible gravity. Just looking at the progression of Japanese culture and aesthetics during the twentieth century will reveal a wide range of Western influence, from the kinds of movies being made to the rising consumption of Western foods.[48] Perhaps that's why so much of mainstream media, from iconography to advertising, penetrates even the most remote pockets of civilization—the sheer volume of it can be heard across the world. In this way, media spreads its tentacular influence like the adventurous spirit of Christopher Columbus, connecting distant regions and mixing cultural influences—and just like Christopher Columbus, it brings horrors to places and cultures totally unprepared for them.

It was an experience thrust upon the citizens of a small province on Viti Levu, Fiji's largest island, who until 1995 hadn't had any exposure to industrialized social standards and mores.[49] At that time, American television was something of a rumor to them —it was present, but rarely seen. Because of that, the island's beauty standards greatly contrasted with those of the industrialized world. So when satellite signals carrying Western programming first hit the region, it was so novel that its assimilation into local norms could be felt everywhere after only three years.

For many people in industrialized countries, a beautiful body is a thin—but not too thin—body, providing a very specific window within which one can be ideally desirable. In contrast, for the people of Viti Levu, to be thick and round is attractive as well as an expression of good health.

In 1995, Dr. Anne E. Becker and her team of Harvard University researchers began conducting a study to measure the impact of this new media on the people consuming it. Sixty-three girls averaging seventeen years old were surveyed in 1995, before the introduction of Western programming, and then another sixty-five were surveyed in 1998, after three years of regular exposure. These residents had access to only one channel broadcasting a limited selection of programming from the United States, Britain, and Australia that included Melrose Place and Beverly Hills 90210.

Sadly, all numbers yielded chilling results: 69 percent of girls surveyed in 1998 said they'd gone on some kind of diet; 29 percent earned a high score on a test measuring risk for eating disorders; and, most tragically, 15 percent admitted to vomiting food to control their weight, compared to 3 percent at the beginning of the study. When interviewed, many of the girls expressed dissatisfaction with their bodies, and several said they were shamed by their friends and social circles because of their weight.

Much like the observations Sabido and company had made in Mexico, for the people of Fiji, it was obvious that television made an impact on their lives—though in their case it was starkly negative. This isn't simply a matter of copycat behavior; this is about how storytelling is powerful enough to strip away time-honored customs. The role of food itself in the history and development of

Fiji is a central and enduring one. Yet the same culture learns to purge food in the name of new standards of aesthetic quality and happiness.

Nine years later, having continued to perform anthropological research on Fiji, Becker returned to Viti Levu to see how time had shaped the region since her study. This time, she sought a larger sample size, providing surveys to 520 girls, 300 of whom gave interviews to supplement the research. The results were even more disheartening: Becker found that 45 percent of girls reported having purged in the past month, and 25 percent admitted to having suicidal thoughts. A contributing factor was the cognitive dissonance central to being a Fijian who wanted to be thin: it was both desired by young people and denounced by the culture at large. Whether they adhered to cultural norms or followed the models they admired on television, impressionable young women ended up being dissatisfied with and criticized for their body weight.[50]

While the Western world has slowly been desensitized to how it consumes these stories and how they alter development, Viti Levu is the sobering wake-up call that the effects are nothing short of significant and the stakes are at times life or death.

Chapter 3

PALATABLE PUBLIC SERVICE ANNOUNCEMENTS

"It is not what you say, it is how you say it," is a phrase we hear often. But nothing can be more accurate than when looking at Social Impact Entertainment. If executed well the story serves up nutrients with the popcorn, that can not only counteract disinformation, but even save lives."

The US Designated Driver Campaign, and the Phrase That Saves Lives

Look. We get it. Everybody has been there. Your Saturday begins innocently and responsibly, checking off your storied list of daily chores, obligations, and priorities, and otherwise committing to being a good, reliable citizen in the face of worldly chaos. And that's exactly when your old friend calls you up and sweet-talks you into the twenty-fifth-birthday bash you completely forgot she was having. Eight hours later, after false promises of sobriety and a few nudges of peer pressure, you are now belting out show tunes while standing on the bar after three college-caliber Long Island iced teas. The point is, you need a ride home, or you and an innocent bystander could meet a grisly end. Good thing you remembered to bring your other friend just in case things took a turn for the reckless.

As much as we take it for granted as a fixture of our culture, the idea of the designated driver isn't just recommended—in a world where ten thousand people are killed in drunk driving accidents every year in the United States alone, it's absolutely essential.[51] The natural question is, what on earth would we have done without it?

We don't need to look very far back to find the answer. The idea isn't nearly as old as we think, nor is it as universal as it should be, considering how long people have been both drinking and driving. On September 10, 1897, only twelve years after the invention of the first commercial automobile, a London cab driver named George Smith crashed his taxi into the side of a building and became the very first person arrested for drunk driving.[52]

When did America adopt the designated driver concept? The idea has its roots in Scandinavia going all the way back to the 1920s but didn't really hit the ground running in America until the late '80s and early '90s; the first campaign promoting it was in 1988.[53]

The question was, how do you get people's attention and get them to follow through? Regulating alcohol hasn't proven effective historically. In fact, Prohibition in the 1920s didn't seem to have much effect beyond arming gangsters and smugglers with new economic frontiers. But between Prohibition's repeal in 1933 and the late 1980s, it seemed that nobody cared to answer the question of how to get people to stop drinking behind the wheel.

In 1987, alcohol-related fatalities in the US had reached 23,626, and in the stately halls of Harvard University boiled an intense desire for change. Unknowingly following in the footsteps of Miguel Sabido's method, William DeJong and Jay A. Winsten—the latter of whom is now an associate dean of the Harvard School of Public Health—began an initiative to depict scenarios involving safer drinking habits in popular television shows in hopes of integrating these habits into mainstream culture.[54] The core idea was to present characters viewers could relate to—series like *Cheers, L.A. Law,* and *The Cosby Show* provided countless examples—as models of beneficial behavior, opening a door for the audience to replicate those behaviors in their daily lives. It was Entertainment-Education in North America, or, as it was named in this specific form, the US Designated Driver Campaign (also known as the Harvard Alcohol Project).

Winsten and DeJong knew they couldn't play things small if they were aiming for maximum impact, so they enlisted the assistance of Hollywood—the big leagues—to give mainstream entertainment entities the chance to make money making a difference. And Hollywood took the bait hook, line, and sinker. It was a cause everyone could get behind, and at no sacrifice to the creative process or the bottom line. Writing teams for prime-time TV shows from giants like ABC, NBC, and CBS were urged to write scripts featuring or mentioning a designated driver, and over four seasons the message was written into the scripts of 160 episodes. Winsten and DeJong knew that if they had at least one connection to each of those networks, they were capable of reaching 75 percent of the American public, depending on the day of the week. That's quite a chunk of the population to sway.

Unlike more passionate campaigns like Mothers Against Drunk Driving (MADD)—largely responsible for pushing drunk driving as a shameful deed, the Harvard Alcohol Project was, despite its name, not anti-alcohol. It didn't need to be. Instead, the campaign opted to persuade drinkers to behave more responsibly by normalizing very slight adjustments in drinking behavior: they wanted to make the bore, or the responsible one, the new life of the party.[55]

One of the biggest social obstacles to overcome was the contrast between the life of the party and responsible drinking. It's also not everybody's first instinct to declare themselves the D.D. when they'd most likely rather be on the receiving end of a funnel. And the desire not to be dismissed as "that guy" or "that woman" outweighs many people's desire to be responsible or even parental. After all, the whole point of a party is to shed your inhibitions—who wants to be a constant reminder to keep them in check?

The aim of the designated driver campaign was to reverse this outlook. You were no longer the damper ruining people's nights—you were the one people could count on, the one who came prepared in case of nuclear fallout.

By the time the campaign was in full swing, beyond the TV shows and networks, Harvard had enlisted the assistance of more than 250 Hollywood professionals. It was the first time three major television networks had collaborated on deploying material working gear-like toward a common goal. To supplement the campaign, the Harvard Alcohol Project also sought to match its prime-time programming with public service announcements advocating for the designated driver. The combo was a one-two punch. By empowering individuals rather than cutting the fun out of their leisure hours, the US Designated Driver Campaign became a quiet cultural movement. Two presidents, George H. W. Bush and Bill Clinton, along with a slew of government agencies and advocacy organizations like Mothers Against Drunk Driving, voiced their support for the campaign. Even the world of sports chimed in, with both the National Basketball Association and Major League Baseball advocating the program.

Within a decade after the initiative began, the concept sank its hooks into the public for good. According to a Roper Poll conducted in 1998, 53 percent of consumers of alcohol claimed to have either used a designated driver or volunteered to be one themselves, and 62 percent of frequent consumers of alcohol claimed they'd taken the same precautions.[56] On an even more celebratory note, recall the number of alcohol-related deaths when the Designated Driver Campaign was launched: 23,626. Within only four years, that number decreased to 17,858, and by 1994, the number had further dropped to 16,580.[57] That's a 30 percent decrease from the campaign's start. In the decade after the campaign launched, Harvard estimated that at least 50,000 lives had been saved.[58] How many of those people had children who didn't have to grow up without parents? How many of those are college students who got to live out the rest of their lives to pursue their dreams? The answer: still not enough.

Further digging reveals that Jay Winsten isn't done yet. His latest campaign is distracted driving—driving while texting, Facebooking, or otherwise staring at a screen rather than through the vehicle's windshield. On several important fronts, the distracted driving problem is as grave—if not more so—as drunk driving simply because of the frequency with which it occurs. Unless you're a hard-core alcoholic, you're not drinking all day, every day, and your delicate liver thanks you immeasurably. But since smartphones became ubiquitous, we've become a culture that's connected to our devices around the clock, seven days a week. And using your device behind the wheel doesn't carry the kind of social stigma of drunk driving. So Winsten is turning once more to mainstream media to aid in his endeavor. He's not there yet, but you have to start somewhere—and this time he has a road map.

Grey's Anatomy

If we trace the career path of series creator and lead writer Shonda Rhimes, *Grey's Anatomy* seems like the intersection of several lifelong ambitions, the seeds of which were planted at a young age. A Black woman who raised six children while attending college and eventually earning a PhD, Rhimes's mother feels like a model for the complex, diverse, and accomplished women Rhimes would write about in her prime. And Rhimes developed ambitions just as lofty as her mother's.

All her life, the hospital was an object of fascination for Rhimes, and she's admitted to being addicted to television surgeries—she and her sister have regularly remarked on the shows they watched and the surgeries they found fascinating.[59] During casual conversation with Rhimes during a hospital visit, a doctor mentioned that it was uncomfortable to shave her legs in the facility showers. This hit Rhimes like lightning—here was a woman who worked such a grueling job that on reflection, it's hardly surprising that she didn't have time elsewhere in her life to tend to something as essential as personal grooming. Rhimes realized she needed to write about women who are driven without being cutthroat and professional without taking themselves too seriously, or in other words, actual human beings with flaws, senses of humor, and competence in their respective hospitals.

But though medicine captured Rhimes's curiosity, it was visual entertainment that captured her passion and evolved into her calling. And as everybody crawling his or her way through the perilous landscape of the entertainment industry knows full well, work hardly ever comes easily right out of the gate. Rhimes's career as a screenwriter began somewhat mixed, beginning with the

HBO television drama *Introducing Dorothy Dandridge* (1999) and continuing with the Britney Spears vehicle *Crossroads* (2002)—which, although critically panned and earning a whopping eight Golden Raspberry nominations, became in its own strange way a precious nostalgia piece of early 2000s cinema (whatever that's worth). Not long after, Rhimes was asked to pen the script for the sequel to the hit Anne Hathaway film *Princess Diaries*. Though that film was once again critically panned, Rhimes looks back fondly on the experience. After all, she did get to work with Julie Andrews, aka *the* Mary Poppins. Even the staunchest critics probably wouldn't have turned down an opportunity that golden if it fell in their laps.

But then came her first television pitch. Rhimes envisioned a show featuring journalists performing war reportage in the Middle East. It was an interesting, timely premise, though its comedic tone was ultimately too ill-fitting for such a sensitive post-9/11 time. But ABC, the multimedia juggernaut that requested the pilot, kept Rhimes in mind, and shortly thereafter requested a new pilot. This was Rhimes's chance. She had ascended the ranks as a scriptwriter, gotten her foot in the door as a television writer, and finally, the door was opening—with *Grey's Anatomy*, she had the perfect project that fit her sensibilities.

The story of *Grey's Anatomy* revolves around the life of Meredith Grey, played by Ellen Pompeo, who is the daughter of a world-renowned surgeon—just the name alone sends murmurs rippling through the show's hospital staff. Meredith's mother urges her not to pursue medicine, but like many children of prosperous parents, the need to take on the mantle gets the better of her. And to her relief and perhaps surprise, she's good at it. But when she becomes an intern at a hospital, her mother's prestige begins to weigh heavily on her. She's very aware that she's her mother's daughter, and so is the hospital staff—in a jealous fit, one of her fellow interns, played by Sandra Oh, accuses her of getting the job only because of her connections.

But that's the dramatic thrust, not necessarily the primary source of interest. Meredith's very first scene—our first image of the show—opens with her unclothed on a couch after we piece together what was a drunken one-night stand. The man on the floor, also naked and also waking up, is Patrick Dempsey, who seems keenly interested in extending his relationship with Meredith. She, however, does not reciprocate and makes it very clear that the fun they both indulged in is officially over, book slammed closed. But then she arrives at the hospital for her first day as an intern, and lo and behold, one of the chief doctors is, in a stunning turn of events, the same man from her drunken one-night stand. The two then spend the rest of the series walking a very fine tightrope of sexual tension—are they keeping things strictly professional, or will things tip over as they did when they first met?

The show's blend of soapy relationships and real-world operating-room tension made for absorbing viewing, and the Internet is flooded with people who claim the series inspired them to pursue a career in medicine. But what sort of real-world impact does a series like *Grey's Anatomy* have on the public's view of medicine? Could a show known for sensationalizing the hospital environment in fact change people's perspective on specific issues of health?

Enter Jennifer Jako, a filmmaker who advocates for literacy on sexually transmitted illnesses like HIV/AIDS. Jako was only eighteen when she tested positive for HIV—she had had six sex partners, and it was a one-night stand with a high school friend that would change her life forever. She gained attention within the HIV/AIDS community for a 1999 documentary called *Blood Lines*, interviewing HIV positive youth around the world about their hopes and fears. Twenty years after the release, Jako now has a child of her own—who has not contracted her mother's condition, thanks to the miracles of modern medicine.

But despite Jako's presence as a positive force within the community, the announcement of her pregnancy in 2006 spurred a certain amount of controversy. It became news when a pregnant Jako was featured in a 2006 *Newsweek* magazine article on AIDS/HIV survivors.[60] The idea that people with the diagnosis could, in fact, have children without transferring their illnesses to offspring was a relatively recent development and wasn't mentioned in the article. As far as general public knowledge was concerned, having a child meant giving your child a death sentence right out of the gate, and Jako received numerous letters expressing outrage that she had behaved so irresponsibly. One woman went so far as to suggest that she should have had an abortion, even though she herself didn't morally believe in it.

Jako knew the public reaction to her pregnancy was a product of misperception, but she was faced with a difficult question: how do you change the narrative on such a controversial and emotionally charged topic for both your community and the public at large?

The answer: charge straight at it with *Grey's Anatomy* and a form of the Sabido Method. The idea came from the Kaiser Family Foundation, who had worked with Jako on producing her wave-making documentary. Kaiser was aware of the miscommunication of facts regarding pregnancy and childbirth in patients with

HIV/AIDS and decided to work hand-in-hand with Jako on an experimental program to inform the public through the very entertainment they consumed so voraciously.

The model was simple: write a small storyline in an episode of the show discussing an HIV-positive pregnant woman, sneak in some facts about the reality of her situation and the new medical options available to her, and add a coating of the show's preestablished threads of romantic plot and interhospital tension.

Jako was even invited into the writer's room to tell her story, and nearly two years after her controversial magazine appearance, she had a fictional avatar gracing the small screen, faced with a real situation from her life, with the show even speaking some of the exact words she used in the writer's room. "I have learned how to live with this, and I never want to bring a child into this world who is infected."[61]

The medical advice the pregnant character receives from show regular Izzie Stevens (Katherine Heigl) was this: "I wasn't telling you there was *some* chance your baby might not be born sick; I was telling you there's a 98 percent chance your baby could be born perfectly healthy. A 98 percent chance. There's a greater chance of your child being born with Down syndrome than there is of you passing HIV on to your child." Subtle? Perhaps not, but that's a small price to pay for an opportunity to adjust people's perspective on an issue concerning life and death.

To prove the efficacy of the experiment, Kaiser conducted a survey before and after the airing. When asked about their opinion on the issue of HIV-positive parents having children, 61 percent initially voted that it was irresponsible. In an identical survey administered after the *Grey's Anatomy* episode aired, that number dropped to 34 percent.[62]

Do experiments like these eliminate the kind of disinformation that caused Jako grief during what should have been one of the best moments of her life? Sadly, no. No matter how hard you try, some people, whether out of legitimate confusion or their own stubbornness, will remain unreachable, no matter how accessible the facts might be. That said, if you make information available to people, even in a form as seemingly innocuous as a high-drama television series, "ignorance" becomes less of an excuse. Not even series creator Shonda Rhimes could have predicted her flagship series would create such positive impact, though it was every bit her intent.

Chapter 4

WHO NEEDS A JOB?

Motivating specific social action is one thing, but the power of storytelling doesn't stop there. It has the potential to influence how people choose to live their entire lives, including what jobs they take. When taking on a professional mantle, some follow in the footsteps of their parents or other mentors, while others are inspired by the media they consume. A study released by UK law firm Fletchers Solicitors in 2017 proved revealing: 39 percent of surveyed youth (ages eighteen to twenty-four) reported that they chose their career path based on the influence of the television shows and movies they were watching—and that number accounts only for those who were conscious of the link.[63] Perhaps media is capable of impacting not only our daily decision-making but also our chosen careers—and thus, our entire lives.

Top Gun

Top Gun: Maverick was the biggest film of 2022, fighting its way up the ranks to become one of the top dozen highest-grossing movies of all time. Thirty-six years ago, the original *Top Gun* (1986) also made quite an impact—but not only at the box office. Taken as a story, the film is essentially a two-hour tribute to the act of flying an F-14. When missions are embarked upon in the movie, we see no insight into the lives or motivations of enemy flyers—

they exist as target practice for our heroes, broadly drawn and so lovingly photographed, the Navy itself might as well have been pulling focus. And on a purely visceral level, this approach works in spades. The very first images on-screen are fighter jets roaring with triumph from the deck of an aircraft carrier, with director Tony Scott drenching everything from ground crew to the Indian Ocean in a mustard tint so intense, it could dramatize a freshly painted wall.

The saturated visuals befit the film's reverent attitude toward the subject matter. In *Top Gun*, to be a pilot isn't simply a paycheck occupation—it is a summons to manhood. And manhood demands definition—to be a man means being your *own* man. That's the primary journey of Tom Cruise's lead character, Maverick, the son of a lauded and legendary pilot, struggling to create his own legacy in the shadow of his father. Through the *Top Gun* flight school, he is given a platform to become the author of his own identity.

This film design isn't an accident. Despite being packed with rip-roaring, mile-high spectacle, the film itself was relatively cheap, with a production budget of only $15 million (roughly $35 million today when adjusted for inflation). Compared to the $200 million blockbusters that have become a summertime staple, that's practically the cost of an indie movie. The low cost was partly due to a bargain struck with the US military to ensure that its image was as rose-tinted and spotless as humanly possible. In exchange for renting authentic planes, pilots, and bases from the government for only $1.8 million, as well as allowing scenes to be filmed in the real-life halls of the TOPGUN flight academy (US Navy Fighter Weapons School), Paramount was required to give the Navy script approval to guarantee that its reputation was upheld in every detail.[64] For example, the death of a major character, Goose, was originally written to be another jet crash, but the Navy was anxious about the number of crashes in the film, so the cause of his demise as changed to a botched evacuation.

The Navy's involvement in production didn't stop there. Although it's illegal for the US Navy to outright endorse a particular service or product, like a movie, loopholes were soon exploited. The Navy established recruiting booths outside or next door to multiplexes screening the film, hoping to hook young firecrackers emerging from the theater on an adrenaline high—as Tom Cruise's Maverick says, "This is what I call a target-rich environment."[65]

The Navy didn't simply want to be cast in a good light. They actively wanted the audience to "feel the need" as much as the characters did, and they wanted to capitalize on the wave they hoped the movie would produce.

Boy, did the wave prove fruitful. The film is among the most financially successful of Tom Cruise's storied career, quickly becoming the highest-grossing film of 1986 and maintaining its opening-week theater count for six straight months.[66] Even the soundtrack sold more than nine million copies. More important than the box-office figures, however, is the effect the film had on young men interested in military service. As was reported in a 1986 *Los Angeles Times* interview with recruiter Lieutenant Commander Laura Marlowe, in the months following the film's summer release, her recruiting office received twice as many phone inquiries about joining the aviation program. Did *Top Gun* play a significant role? Well, as always, that question is a multiheaded beast, but when asked about their motivations for signing up, 90 percent of new applicants said they had seen the film.[67]

Whatever your opinion of *Top Gun* as a piece of filmmaking, the movie was polished by its makers and financiers to ensure it provided the visceral outlet both its characters and audiences strived for. If the string-pullers behind the scenes intended audiences to "feel the need," their efforts clearly worked, forever changing the career paths and lives of a significant number of people.

The Wolf of Wall Street

As great as it would be for the world to operate as a gently boiling pot of wholesome pursuit, not all inspiration comes from a divine source, and that includes the movies. From gangsters enthralled by the lurid spectacle of *Scarface* to drug enthusiasts banging the drum over *Fear and Loathing in Las Vegas*, sometimes movies can, in their attempts to portray a job or activity in an entertaining way, end up swaying their audience in favor of the thing they're attempting to subtly undermine. Hard to come up with a better example than the multi–Academy Award–nominated *The Wolf of Wall Street.*

As an artistic achievement and piece of entertainment, director Martin Scorsese's three-hour rush of a movie is a masterpiece of coded excess, a kind of first-person portrait of the world and the allures of confidence men and the monstrous people they can be beneath the slick veneer of charm and persuasion. A long-time passion project for star Leonardo DiCaprio, it features some of the most electric and momentous filmmaking from a director who had just recently cracked the seventy-year mark, and the ease and precision with which editor Thelma Schoonmaker filters so many characters and bits of information through her kinetic filter is unparalleled in her towering career. The film had a peculiar production history, switching both production companies and directors, with Ridley Scott attached to direct the film for Warner Brothers two years before Scorsese's big-budget independent production was given the green light.

The story of the film charts the rise, peak, and ultimate downfall of Jordan Belfort, a Wall Street stockbroker played by DiCaprio who begins the movie as a complete greenhorn to the world of finance. He's introduced to his boss, Mark Hanna, played in brilliantly charismatic fashion by Matthew McConaughey, who welcomes him into the shark tank of a Wall Street call center, bursting with a flurry of telephones, frustration-fueled vulgarities, and the high-wire tension of the driven environment. Hanna takes Belfort out to lunch and, in ways that go beyond inappropriate almost immediately, essentially tells him, in the midst of a cocaine-fueled pep talk for the ages, to shamelessly screw over his clients in pursuit of as much commission as he can get his hands on. Belfort eventually loses his job after a devastating market crash, but—inspired by Hanna's lunch—decides to keep moving forward, landing himself a job at a penny stock firm.

We soon see that Belfort is such a preternaturally gifted salesman that he could sell water to a fish and salt to a slug. He sells penny stocks, essentially worthless shares in the tiniest, most ramshackle start-up companies imaginable, by pitching them as tremendous. Each client ends up buying way too much of way too little, and Belfort gets a fat check. Building from this philosophy and the coworkers who want in, a new firm, Stratton Oakmont, is born, and what follows is the creation of an empire of deceit adorned with hookers, cocaine, Quaaludes, yachts, luxury foods, trophy wives, and pretty much any other expression of material decadence one can imagine. All achieved via off-screen and out-of-sight ordinary citizens, too naively focused on their own pursuit of the American dream to know when they are being conned.

That either sounds incredibly appealing or morally bankrupt, depending on who you are and what your values happen to be. The film is itself a drama on Quaaludes that ends with our heroes basically escaping with very little consequence, a depressing portrait of one of the developed world's most consistent problems: rich men with too much money and not enough accountability. In an interview with the YouTube channel DP/30, editor Schoonmaker made the intentions of the filmmaking team very clear: "If you want to be like these people, then I don't know what to say."[68]

And it's a good thing she won't waste her breath, because alarmingly enough, plenty of people walked out of Scorsese's opus with something of the wrong impression. According to a report conducted internally by the job listing aggregator Indeed.com, around the time *The Wolf of Wall Street* was hitting theaters and permeating the public conversation, job searches for stockbroker positions rose 79.6 percent in the United States and 44 percent in the UK.[69] What could the reason be? How could some walk away from the movie needing a scalding shower while a great number of others walked away fired up and ready for their new careers?

The answer may be in the DNA of not just a movie, but the original story it was telling. The fact of the matter is, no matter how deceitful and cold-blooded their methods for making money were, these men used that money to have unchained, irresponsible fun, and the film depicted exactly that. As the expression goes: YOLO.

Within the first five minutes, we observe DiCaprio, once a matinee idol of pedestal innocence, snorting cocaine off a prostitute's backside. For a culture as steeped in capitalism as ours, that turned out to be a far more desirable scenario than the filmmakers anticipated. But it wasn't from a lack of trying. While Belfort gets off with a relatively light punishment of two years in prison (which the film depicts as a fluffy oasis of tennis courts and leisure), Scorsese and team make certain to show that there is no happy ending for anyone else in this world. It is as if the fable says, choose this life of greed and you will end up in jail, strung-out, or dead by murder or suicide. Yet it is in the nuances of the story, on a cerebral level, that this lesson is learned. Meanwhile, and this is true of screenings around Wall Street at the time, traders cheered the on-screen antics, invoking an interesting question about the power of modeling and representing behavior in a film in a monkey-see, monkey-do fashion versus in an intellectual manner. What has the biggest impact on behavior?

Chapter 5

MEDIA MIMICRY: THE SIDE EFFECTS OF MODELING

"Television is the retina of the mind's eye," says Professor Brian O'Blivion in one of the more controversial movies of the 1980s, David Cronenberg's *Videodrome* (1983). The quote specifies television, but one can take its message even further: media, in all of its forms, becomes a filter through which we push our own experiences, and in turn it colors our reality. If we see a scenario or a behavior on television, in a movie, or even in a comic book, we're seeing something fake that gives us a sense of very real catharsis. And as Albert Bandura demonstrated, when children see images that provoke violence or aggression, they can be compelled to replicate the behaviors they see. That's not true of just kids. If Sabido and Bandura proved anything, it's that even in adults, images in the media can be models of behavior, both positive and negative. Throughout recent history, one can leaf through a slew of examples of people taking the entertainment they consume as a model to adhere to, sometimes to violent and deadly ends. Here are just a few.

Superman

Not all calls to action lead to the most heroic of outcomes, just as not all heroes inspire the right kind of behavior.

A question: was there a child growing up in the past century who wasn't spellbound by Superman? He's not just a person who flew, leapt tall buildings, and occasionally rescued the terminally imperiled Lois Lane—Superman is appealing because he's a symbol for the best humankind can aspire to, a pure spirit applying his alien abilities to uphold our brightest ideals with unyielding commitment.

But kids of a certain age don't necessarily think that deeply about the content they enjoy. To them, being like Superman likely means melting steel by shooting laser beams from their eyes, thwarting bad guys with strength and wit, and flying the circumference of the globe with such speed that time itself reverses and innocent people are brought back from the dead. Because children are vulnerable to mimicking the behavior of their on-screen idols, they are (rather unfortunately) good case studies to highlight the power of monkey-see, monkey-do modeling—and storytellers might consider this impact in their prose.

Following the inception of the *Superman* comics, in Columbus, Ohio, an eight-year-old boy named Larry King wound up in the hospital after donning a homemade costume and jumping from a second-story fire escape. When questioned at his bedside, Larry admitted that he'd hoped the wind would carry him through the air, just like Superman. A nearly identical example came in the form of James Henderson, also eight years old, who sprained his ankle in Des Moines, Iowa, after draping himself in a cape and leaping from the second floor of his apartment building.[70]

There are more tragic examples further along the caped hero's timeline. In December 1978, Richard Donner released his hallmark film version of *Superman*, boldly bearing the tagline "You will believe a man can fly."[71] This belief gripped four-year-old Charles Green of Brooklyn, New York, who was taken to see the film by his father soon after release. According to his mother, in the days after, Charles could be seen hoisting himself on top of tables, chairs, and beds to leap heroically into the air like Superman. In a heartbreaking turn, Charles tried the same stunt from the ledge of a seventh-floor apartment window, remaining in a coma for nine days before finally succumbing to his injuries on February 11, 1979.[72]

Decades later, in the spring of 2001, during an unsupervised water balloon fight between neighborhood kids, a nine-year-old third-grader named Julian Roman leaped from the top floor of a Bronx apartment complex in hopes of landing on the rooftop next door, hitting an air-conditioning unit on the way down and finally dying from internal bleeding just a few hours later. His last words before taking flight? "Look, I'm Superman!"[73]

George Reeves, who from 1952 to 1958 played Superman in the first TV show based on the character, saw the impact the character and the TV series were making and adjusted his public image accordingly. He quit smoking and consuming alcohol at public events, and he attempted to persuade the publishers of Superman comics to stop selling Superman's iconic red-and-blue suit to kids. In the words of Jay Emmett, who was responsible for licensing Superman-related merchandise, "We couldn't have kids buying costumes if they were going to jump out the window."[74]

Stories like this exist ad nauseam, not just for Superman but for movies and television everywhere in regard to their effect on developing minds. It's why we have the Motion Picture Association of America and a rating system on everything from video games to music. Young minds are the most impressionable.

So what then about storytelling that influences more fully blossomed minds?

Fight Club: Rules 1 and 2 Do Not Apply

"With a gun barrel between your teeth, you speak only in vowels."[75]

If you don't know that line by heart, you probably didn't grow up in the '90s. If there's one film that exemplified the shifting social tides of that era, it was David Fincher's beautifully chaotic masterpiece, *Fight Club*. The movie combines one of the biggest stars in the world, Brad Pitt, with one of the most iconoclastic directors, David Fincher, and a story as primally felt as it is intelligently disturbing.

Based on the novel of the same name by transgressive fiction writer Chuck Palahniuk, the film is perhaps known equally for its fiendishly devoted cult fan base and for its reputation as a piece of art. The film notably bombed at the box office when it was released in the autumn of 1999, a year that was rife with bold, risk-taking cinema like *The Matrix*, *American Beauty*, and Paul Thomas Anderson's *Magnolia*. While those films enjoyed a certain amount of Awards-season buzz that cemented their success, *Fight Club*, arguably the blackest sheep in a year seemingly designed for black sheep, received hardly any love whatsoever until it found its way into the home video market, where listless high schoolers and scruffy college students could discover it for themselves and obsess over it until the tape wore out.

The story centers around an unnamed narrator who suffers from what looks like the most mind-numbing insomnia ever experienced, losing himself in the droning rhythms of his office-bound, workaday lifestyle. He's looking for something to either help him sleep or bring the variety he needs to break himself from the waking dream his daily routine has become. He tries everything from reinventing his apartment with the help of a catalog to attending cancer-support groups and pretending to be deathly ill, but nothing works. Until he's on a plane one day, and next to him sits a leather-clad embodiment of all the masculine freedom he's ever dreamed of: Tyler Durden, a soap salesman with a black heart and a seductive streak. He's everything a conventional man might aspire to be: he's good looking, he's endlessly confident, and he has a lack of self-awareness that enables him to pursue anything headlong and without fear.

After an exchange that utterly captivates our main character, Durden hands our narrator his business card, something that comes in handy when his apartment explodes and he needs a last-minute place of temporary residence. From here, they start spending time together hopping from bar to bar, place to place. And then it happens: Tyler, without a hint of irony, asks the narrator to punch him as hard as he can. Our protagonist is dumbfounded: surely he can't be serious? But Tyler goads him into a violent burst, something the narrator admits brings a certain amount of thrill and catharsis.

From this fight grows a string of fights, all for the purpose of exhausting the fighters' anger and pent-up tensions. People watch Tyler and the narrator, first in horror, then in fascination. Spectators form, and eventually, a man asks, "Can I be next?" That's how the story gets its title: these fights turn into underground meetings of frustrated men who clobber each other into blood puddings just to feel like they're alive and in control of their lives again. But there's a slippery slope developing, one into which all the members of Tyler Durden's club find themselves falling. It starts with Fight Club, and then it turns into picking fights with strangers in the street. Which turns into acts of anarchy to protest the advertising world's method of emasculating men for the purposes of marketing. Which turns into minor terrorist threats. Which turns into trucks of explosive gelatin ready to detonate and bring down skyscrapers across an entire city.

This flirtation with anarchy is what makes *Fight Club* so powerful and what makes it such a controversial movie even after its reappraisal. What begins as a celebration of the liberation of masculinity slowly reveals itself as a message far more intelligent: how conventional views of masculinity are, in their purest and least monitored form, inherently self-destructive, and can lead to violent and sociopathic mindsets and behaviors.

At least, that's what *Fight Club* was *supposed* to be about. Not only was that slippery slope mistaken for an endorsement of violence by many critics, including the usually perceptive Roger Ebert (he gave it only two stars out of the coveted four), but many of the audience members who love the movie have, to this day, misunderstood the hero worship at the center of the film. We're meant to be seduced by Tyler Durden so that once the terrorism comes into play, we feel complicit in the toxic masculinity the film is critiquing. But instead, some sectors of *Fight Club*'s fan base worship the guy without reflection, chanting his mantra like psalms from a religious text. And sadly, this spills over into mimicking some of *Fight Club*'s most disturbing scenarios as if they're expressions of virtue.

For proof of this, look no further than the number of amateur Fight Clubs (as if there are professional Fight Clubs) that have sprung up in the twenty years since the film was released, especially those consisting of young men.

In 2000 a man named Gints Klimanis, a software engineer and martial arts instructor, started a network of young men—mostly in their twenties and thirties and working in the tech industry—who met regularly in Menlo Park, congregating in a garage in this bedroom community of San Francisco to conduct knock-down, drag-out, bare-knuckle fights until somebody screamed uncle.[76]

Much like in *Fight Club*, once they'd all beaten each other to a pulp, they'd go back to work in the morning, giving presentations and getting bleached by computer monitor backlights as if nothing had happened the night before. When the constituents were interviewed and pressed for their motivations, one man, Shiyin Siou, said, "This is as close as you can get to a real fight, even though I'd never been in one."[77] He also admitted to having fantasies about hurting people. If you've seen the film, that motivation sounds frighteningly familiar: "I felt like destroying something beautiful," the narrator declares.

Another club member, Dinesh Prasad, who had been attending the meetups for five years, admitted that he'd once skipped his wedding anniversary to attend the Fight Club. An NPR story from 2006 reported that a number of different Fight Clubs were started by teens in the mid-2000s, in Arlington, Texas, with the filming of the fights (and subsequent underground sale of the videos) becoming something of a staple of the ritual.[78]

Sounds harmless, right? Sure, barbaric and strange, but there's nothing inherently wrong with consenting adults agreeing to beat the lights out of each other on private property. But here's where things began to get truly disturbing: there are numerous examples of young people emulating the terrorist acts into which Tyler Durden's revolution devolves, sometimes in lockstep with the fictional trademarks. In 2002, a young man named Lucas John Helder was apprehended on suspicion of being connected to eighteen incidents of planting pipe bombs.[79] The bombs were planted in five states, all intended to form the shape of a smiley face across the map of the United States.[80] In *Fight Club* the same smiley face was used to mark the place vandalized by the members of Project Mayhem, a larger group that evolved from Tyler Durden's *Fight Club*.

Of course the easy thing to say here is, well, that's life; people are always going to misinterpret, or some crazy person will respond to a story without rhyme or reason and there's no stopping that. That is true, but not entirely. The violence in *The Matrix* and the shooters' copycat black trench coats didn't lead to the Columbine High School shooting.[81] While all three assailants said they were influenced by the book *The Catcher in the Rye*, this didn't result in the murders of Rebecca Schaeffer and John Lennon or the assassination attempt on Ronald Reagan.[82] But it is also true that exposure to certain ways of being can risk begetting similar moral attitudes in some viewers through desensitization that is real and transmutable, which leads to the inevitable question for all storytellers: what kinds of stories do you want to tell?

Chapter 6

POPULATION MEDIA CENTER: BILL RYERSON

In the first chapter, we explored the genesis of the Sabido Method and how statistically significant its results were throughout Mexico. Sabido set out to have an impact, used storytelling in tandem with social programs, and had a quantifiable cultural effect. But could this methodology be enacted by others in distant locations, in other tongues, and in a myriad of formats? One organization built on Sabido's Method set out to ask that very question.

Since his years as a university student in the late '60s, Bill Ryerson has made the issue of human population growth his personal mission. He began his academic career studying biology at Amherst College and then attended graduate school at Yale, where he conducted research on insect behavior. Ryerson's thesis advisor at Yale, Charles Remington, one of the most influential figures in modern entomology, invited fellow scientist Paul Ehrlich, a fellow entomologist and professor of biology at Stanford University, to speak at the campus about an issue Ehrlich had recently thrown his focus onto: population. At the time, Ehrlich and his wife, Anne Ehrlich, had just published a landmark book called *The Population Bomb*[83] that explored the causes and impacts of the ballooning human population worldwide.

What struck Ryerson as most compelling in the Ehrlichs' project was the relationship between the skyrocketing number of human beings and the subsequent reduction of habitats vital to other species—the more space required for us to occupy the Earth comfortably, the less space and resources were available for the rest of life on Earth. Together with an attorney, the scientists founded a program called Zero Population Growth in 1968,[84] an initiative to create a balance between the number of people being born and the number of people expiring, while at the same time creating a balance between coexisting species.

This goal ignited a fire in Ryerson that would blaze a trail toward his remaining career. The year after Zero Population Growth was founded, Ryerson gathered a conglomerate of over 200 like-minded students into the fourth ZPG chapter in the country with the goal of empowering people to live healthier and more prosperous lives across the globe. At first, the organization was isolated to the university, and one of its first big missions was to cement the first Earth Day initiatives on the Yale campus. The initiatives were a success, landing the students in a feature for *Life* magazine's Earth Day Issue. This work soon eclipsed Ryerson's interest in insect biology and drove him to turn activism into his full-time job.

The aspect of the issue that Ryerson has championed most strongly is the impact of family planning on population growth, not just in the US but also in less developed parts of the world. It wouldn't shock anybody to learn that too many people in the US are having children due to a lack of proper precaution and contraception—but to a great number of people, especially within the more fanatical circles of the Christian right, the topic of contraception is just an excuse to market sexual activity to young adults.

In Ryerson's eyes, lack of reproductive health knowledge is one of the root causes of population overgrowth, and this makes sense: the less people know regarding the prevention of pregnancy, the more babies, wanted or otherwise, will be produced as a result. Lack of pregnancy management also poses dangers for women across the world: A reported 295,000 women died in 2017 from complications related to pregnancy or childbirth,[85] including severe bleeding and infections. Even more alarming is that 44 percent of pregnancies worldwide are unplanned and 22 percent are unwanted.[86] By providing points of entry toward contraceptive and family planning measures, results would not just slow the rate of population growth—it would literally save lives.

After stints at Population Institute, two Planned Parenthood affiliates, and Population Communications International, Ryerson took up these insights and set out to reenact Miguel Sabido's method by founding Population Media Center in 1998. His success was almost instantaneous and global, most notably his popular series for Hulu, *East Los High*. The plot of each season centers around a group of students at a predominantly Latino high school buried in the outskirts of Los Angeles, all tackling the challenges many adolescents face on the road to responsible adulthood: sex, teen pregnancy, gang violence, and so on. The central character in Season 1, Jessie, navigates adolescence through gaining a boyfriend named Jacob, experiencing sex for the first time (opting out of the "Virgin's Club"), and dealing with her long-lost cousin, who is introduced as a runaway stealing drugs to sell just to escape a horrible living situation.

We hardly know who these characters are before they start copulating with and cheating on each other. The plots lines are juicier than freshly cut steaks and about as entertaining as that sounds. For all its soapy trappings, though, the show's production value appears higher than average, and its English-language format allows the series to cross cultural barriers in ways telenovelas simply don't. Unbeknownst to its core audience, *East Los High* was an adaptation of Sabido's Method of inducing social change.

The series ran between 2013 and 2017, producing four seasons totaling 61 episodes, all currently available on Hulu. In that regard, the series pushes the Sabido Method into the twenty-first century by wedding it with modern revolutions in content consumption. If the future of television broadcasting is streaming services like Netflix, Amazon Prime, and Hulu, why not make it the future of social change in the same swing.

Teen pregnancy is one issue the series was designed to tackle. According to a 2012 study performed by the United Nations Population Fund, only 38 percent of teens in Latin American countries used condoms during their first sexual experience.[87] A report by the Centers for Disease Control and Prevention found that in 2017, the birthrate among US Latina girls aged fifteen to nineteen was more than twice that of white teenagers.[88] How successful was *East Los High* as an Entertainment-Education initiative?

Two of the show's researchers and consultants, Hua (Helen) Wang and Arvind Singhal, designed a simple but revealing experiment to track how the audience of *East Los High* was responding to its motivated content.[89] They surveyed 136 Latina students at the University of Texas at El Paso to gain insight on their knowledge of reproductive health and various family planning options, including condom use, then separated them into several groups for individual exposure. One group was given fake news stories; another group was given the plot of an episode of *East Los High* condensed into a short story; another group watched episodes of the series itself; and another group watched episodes of the series coupled with the supplementary materials available online, including makeup tutorials, mini PSA-style information videos about the issues in the show, and deleted scenes. Once all the groups had digested the materials, they were given post-tests to see how their perspectives had changed.

The test found that of these groups, the one that watched both the series and the extras had learned the most about reproductive health measures; the one that watched only the show learned more but not quite as much as the previous group; and the one that read fake news hadn't changed enough to even blip the radar.[90]

Looking to the numbers, the day *East Los High* first aired, visits to the website StayTeen.org, a public teen-pregnancy prevention initiative, doubled. In the first month after the show debuted, 27,000 people used the Planned Parenthood widget from the *East Los High* website—55 percent of these users were brand new, and 81 percent of viewers shared and advocated the resources they discovered through the program.[91] The evidence makes a strong case for the show's efficacy: the more absorbed people become in a show and in its ideas, the more compelled they are to retain and act on the information with which it's loaded. This is one of the central pillars of the Sabido Method at work: when people develop a personal connection to the characters and their world, they are more likely to model their own behavior after them.

Population Media Center's ambitions stretch globally, far beyond English-speaking territories. Another of their series, *Último Año*, sought to achieve a kind of success similar to that of *East Los High*, again aimed at teen pregnancy and family-planning options—but this time via MTV Latin America. We've explored in earlier chapters how Miguel Sabido was able to help curb overpopulation through telenovelas, and although he made a tremendous impact, the underlying issue still exists and needs to be addressed.

In an attempt to keep its results laser-focused on its goal of social change, Population Media Center worked with the producers of *Último Año* and trained the series' entire creative crew on the Sabido Method, particularly on how to weave educational messages into storylines that empower positive decision-making rather than having characters exposit those ideas like a visual op-ed. Assaulting people with information turns people off; opening a door through an empathetic connection turns people on.

In conjunction with the series, Population Media Center launched an initiative called the SexySex campaign to allow interested viewers to find out more about the characters' behavior.[92] This included both Internet and SMS-based notification services providing further insight into contraceptive options, along with a website connecting viewers to resources like family-planning centers and a series of PSAs featuring the cast providing information on the issues discussed in each episode.

Último Año centers around the students of a high school, albeit a more exclusive and affluent one than the populace of *East Los High*. The main character, Benjamín, hosts a foreign exchange student named Martín, and although they begin as friends, the loyalties and betrayals that are the series' lifeblood soon kick into high gear, and high drama sets in like paranoia. While *Último Año* wouldn't have quite the universal appeal of *East Los High*, which was accessible to English-speaking countries, fluent Spanish-speaking audiences turned out in droves. Airing for an hour a day, five nights a week, the series accomplished an audience reach of nearly twenty-two million people across Latin America.

So we return to our immortal question: how was the impact measurable? Of the surveyed viewers of the series, 78 percent of people who had seen *Último Año* reported that they had taken contraceptive measures in the previous month, compared to 64 percent of nonviewers. Surveys also revealed that 95 percent of viewers were more inclined to assist disabled people who were being discriminated against—another central theme in the series—in contrast to 86 percent of nonviewers. Clearly *Último Año* gave awareness of these issues a bit of a bump.

Let's explore one more of Population Media Center's programs. On the list of countries the average Westerner thinks about on a daily basis, Niger likely isn't near the top, but it's arguably the most significant country in terms of the world's population growth.[93] Historically, Niger has had one of the highest fertility rates in the world, always in excess of about 7 children per woman.[94] For context, the fertility rates of the US, China, and India are 1.9, 1.6, and 2.3, respectively. Niger's population is slated to almost triple over the next thirty years, jumping from 23 million in 2019 to a potential 66 million in 2050.[95] That's an enormous outpouring of people onto a planet that has fewer resources to support them each passing day. But Population Media Center knows that enhancing gender equality, child protection, and reproductive health and rights is the way to address this problem. The solution began with another Entertainment-Education initiative, this time in the form of a radio drama in Niger called *Gobe da Haske*, translated as *Tomorrow Will Be a Brighter Day* from its recorded language of Hausa.[96]

Highlighting how overpopulation can lead to neglect and

exploitation of children, Population Media Center's program centered on a very disturbing issue: child trafficking. The story is driven by a mosaic of characters, including a young boy named Kokari stranded in an impoverished existence in Niger. He is lured into working for a charismatic entrepreneur named Katakore who secretly enslaves children into child labor, eventually making Kokari one of his victims. Also present in the drama is Batata, a financially ruined man who is driven through desperation to begin trafficking children on behalf of Katakore, and a young girl named Takirki, who is sold off to a significantly older man in a forced marriage. The series began broadcasting in February 2006 and continued for 144 episodes, each about fifteen minutes long, until January 2007. At the end of the broadcast, a survey was distributed to measure the impact of the series.[97]

With a sample size of 1230 respondents, the results of the survey painted a convincing picture:

1. 39 percent of surveyed listeners knew of at least three family planning options, contrasted with 10 percent of nonlisteners.
2. 23 percent of listeners understood how utilization of family planning could impact child labor and exploitation, contrasted with 6 percent of nonlisteners.
3. 67 percent of listeners were aware of the existence of child labor, as opposed to 28 percent of nonlisteners.
4. 55 percent of listeners were aware of the trafficking of children within Niger, compared to 28 percent of nonlisteners.
5. 34 percent of listeners could list at least three pipelines

into exploitative child labor, compared to 15 percent of nonlisteners.

6. 29 percent of people tuning in could list three gateways into the trafficking of children, contrasted with 14 percent of nonlisteners.
7. And lastly, perhaps most important to raising awareness, 40 percent of those surveyed reported that they had discussed child exploitation with somebody in the past twelve months—a grave difference compared to 19 percent of nonlisteners.[98]

Population Media Center is one of the farthest-reaching endeavors of its kind, assisting in the production of content across mediums in more than fifty countries across the globe, with a combined audience of over 500 million people. Its mission persists.

The world population continues to balloon, currently measuring 8 billion and increasing by more than 80 million every year. The United Nations projects that by 2030 it will reach 8.5 billion, and by 2100 it will be nearly 11 billion.[99] These are alarming numbers by anybody's standards. Enormous, global problems that require reaching a global audience—and how better to do that? The Sabido Method writ large.

Chapter 7

WILL & GRACE: HOMOSEXUALITY IN THE AMERICAN LIVING ROOM

Any great work starts with a dream, and a dream certainly came to vivid life when two writers formed the creative and entrepreneurial bond that would produce *Will & Grace*.

Max Mutchnick first collaborated with David Kohan on the short-lived sitcom *Boston Common* (1996–97). From the ashes of that series arose a new inspiration. The pair concocted an idea about a man and a woman living together, with neither party being attracted to the other, struggling to hold their heads up in New York City. Though NBC initially rejected their pitch, Mutchnick—an openly gay man—and Kohan continued to expand, develop, and refine their idea until in 1997, executives came to their senses, and the two finally hit the ground running with their most enduring property.

The premise is fertile ground for situational comedy, and for ten years, the show lived up to its promise. At the start of the series, Grace (Debra Messing), an interior decorator living in New York City, is thrown into a crossroads when her boyfriend spontaneously pops the question. At first, Grace agrees, but her friend Will, a gay attorney living the single life in the kind of New York apartment that sadly only exists in sitcoms, encourages her not to pursue the marriage if she isn't completely devoted. So Grace takes

Will's advice, and in a classic *uh-oh* scenario, leaves her beloved at the altar in a moment of transcendent self-acceptance, showing up at Will's office in her bridal whites. The glow of the moment soon wears off, however, and she's left in dire straits without a place to live. After receiving help from Will in getting back on her feet, she comes up with an idea that would change America forever: she moves in with Will, thus setting the stage for one of the most popular and widely revered sitcoms in history.

Soon into the series, the cast expands to include two new regulars, just as essential to the chemistry of the show as the titular ones: Karen (Megan Mullally), a friend of Grace and a well-connected social butterfly whose larger-than-life attitude would become one of the primary draws of the show; and Jack (Sean Hayes), also a gay man, and best friend to Will, who faces his own chaotic goings-on with equal parts desperation and the kind of catty detachment that produces endless soundbites.

Although they began as supporting characters, doodles on the outskirts of the show's main plot, Karen and Jack were so appealing they eventually occupied almost equal screen time to the main characters. The infectious interplay among these four as we followed them through their difficulties in navigating a stable adult life would fuel the series for an eight-season initial run, followed by an equally popular revival eleven years after the original series concluded.

One of the essential components that made *Will & Grace* work as a cultural vehicle was the fact that it was a comedy before anything else. If you take a look at the history of mainstream entertainment, from Hollywood movies to family-friendly daytime television viewing, the discussion of homosexuality had been primarily relegated to victim-oriented narratives in which our protagonist experienced shameful discrimination, caught an illness like HIV/AIDS, or struggled with repressed sexuality coming through in very self-destructive forms. So how, then, do storytellers expand perspectives on behaviors that are steeped in stigma?

The writers of *Will & Grace* dove in headfirst. Rather than presenting the American populace with a story of gay struggle, they immersed their gay characters in the day-to-day New York hustle-and-bustle that mainstream media's largest target demographic—white, middle-class America—recognized as its own. The show does not turn its characters' sexualities into bullet points in an impassioned visual essay—rather, they become a source of at times risqué but mostly innocent and good-natured humor, neither celebrated nor condemned. Like the heterosexual women of the story, Will and Jack are simply working to make something comfortable and idyllic out of their restless lives.

Mirroring the Sabido Method in crucial ways, *Will & Grace* presents the audience with a range of behavioral models—only in this case, the goal of the series wasn't explicitly to convince or to empower audiences toward a specific action; it was simply to humanize.

In its leads, the series establishes two representations of homosexual male behavior. In Will, we have the ideal of the publicly acceptable gay male: he's smart; his loyalty as a friend is intense and enduring; and he seeks out stable, monogamous romantic relationships. He's also clean-cut; he's lacking in some of the stereotypical mannerisms attributed to gay people; and he is skilled in a high-competency, high-salary job. Were he straight, he's someone you can imagine viewers would hope their daughter would lock down. Whenever Grace is in peril, whether it's a work-related circumstance or a romantic possibility, Will's voice of reason shines through the shenanigans of which Jack and Karen make meals.

Jack serves as a counterpoint to Will in virtually every character trait. In contrast to Will's security and clarity of mind, Jack is petty, superficial, and often promiscuous. He has no career prospects to speak of and lacks the academic success that brings so much integrity to Will. Jack is the chaos the audience both identifies with and decries. He drifts in and out of situations, peeking in as if to test the air—and oftentimes, he forgets to pull his head out fast enough and ends up in awkward predicaments.

The same contrast exists between the two female leads. Although Grace begins the series in search of direction, she encapsulates everything modern America expects out of adult women: she's financially successful in a field that requires as much creative ingenuity as it does professionalism, and like Will, she seeks out monogamous relationships, strives for stability, and otherwise maintains what most would consider a healthy lifestyle. Meanwhile, Karen is the flip side. She's shamelessly flirtatious, impulsive, and often careless in her endeavor to have a great time regardless of consequence.

While *Will & Grace* is bold in presenting the lives of gay people casually, it does so by using these lives as poster children for rather conventional Western values. That isn't to say that the characters aren't fleshed out beyond that, or that the series betrays their sexualities—in many ways, it doesn't. Gay sex is treated as liberally as heterosexual sex, and both Jack and Will are depicted as being reliable friends in spite of the antics that often come tethered to them. But the values of the series are the values of mainstream

America— the show is designed to require minimal effort or reflection to accept the characters. The fact that Jack and Will are gay is deliberately treated as an afterthought, humanized with charm and a strong dose of humor, plot, and episodic intrigue.

Because of its adherence to these conventions, the series has garnered just as much flak as praise, with some skeptics of the show arguing that in presenting Jack so colorfully, the writers actually do perpetuate negative stereotypes about gay people—flamboyance, sexual deviance, promiscuity, and a relatively erratic way of life, with even Will occasionally devolving into the stereotypical screaming queen for comedic effect in moments of distress. The argument the skeptics make is that because the series is tailored for a mainstream sensibility, the characters and their behavior do nothing but cement the preconceptions audiences have about gay people. Regardless of one's love for the series, there's a nugget of truth there. In fact, going further, one can see the potential danger such portrayals pose to the collective perception of homosexuality—by depicting gay people as being at odds with conventional ideas of manhood, the biased eye might begin to see homosexuality as inherently emasculating. In the minds of a tragic many people, being a gay man makes you less of a man, and though *Will & Grace* laughs with its characters rather than at them, it never actively challenges you to change the way you perceive them—it simply allows you to get comfortable with them.

It will always be challenging to weigh the relative benefits and harms of complex, nuanced issues of perception and behavior, but an argument can be made that there was great value in creating a show that invited a gay guy into viewers' living rooms and made this feel commonplace.

Looking at how the series fared with audiences provides further insight. In a period when gay marriage was illegal in the United States, when two consenting adult men or women in love were not regarded by the state as legitimate, how did the show do on prime time?

When the series debuted, taking up a Monday night slot on NBC, it garnered an average of 12.3 million viewers for the season, a fair opening for a show that was only just generating its viewer base.[100] Even when the show shifted to Tuesday nights in its second season, it still kept its 12 million viewers. But when Season 3 of the series moved to Thursday and gained *Friends* as its lead-in, it catapulted to trendsetting status, earning an average of 17.3 million viewers for two seasons in a row, making *Will & Grace* one of the top twenty series on television. Eleven years later, the success of the series would inspire a revival, a trend set by other popular series of the time like *Gilmore Girls* and, of all things, *The X-Files*.

In an appearance on the NBC talk show *Meet the Press* in 2012, vice president Joe Biden openly credited *Will & Grace* with shaping perceptions of homosexuality in America: "When things really begin to change, is when the social culture changes," the VP said, elaborating on his gradually shedding unease toward gay marriage. "I think 'Will and Grace' probably did more to educate the American public than almost anything anybody's ever done so far. And I think—people fear that which is different. Now they're beginning to understand."[101] The fact that an authority figure as high up as the vice president—particularly one who wasn't always in favor of gay marriage himself—attributed impact and change to the show is a thing of beauty all its own.

Despite decades if not centuries of progress, homosexuality is still a significant point of contention. To this day, cultures across the world, from Africa to the Middle East, continue to publicly condemn and ostracize people for their sexuality, with some countries such as Iran even putting citizens to death for being gay. Even in America, the land of the free, there are still pockets that equate homosexuality and pedophilia, as insane as that sounds. So imagine how bold it was at the turn of the century, twenty years ago, to put these marginalized lives right in the crosshairs of public view—and not only to have the series take, but to have it take off like an Olympic sprinter. Sometimes representing and humanizing can be a revolution unto itself.

Chapter 8

EARLY AUTEURS: THE GOOD, THE BAD, AND THE UGLY

Mainstream storytelling, to say the least, has been gravely lacking in three-dimensional portraits of minorities. Tracing the history of minority representation in film is both surprising and troubling. This chapter is about the bad along with the good, and how what not to do led to even more of what not to do.

Let's begin by looking at an early and notable example plucked from one of Hollywood history's foremost cornerstones: the sweeping romantic epic *Gone with the Wind* (1939). Beyond its stories of troubled production—the film endured a revolving door of directors hired and fired by producer David O. Selznick—the film has been revered by critics for its scope, artistry, and even dialogue—"Frankly, my dear, I don't give a damn"[102]—ripping through time. But beneath the satisfaction of the film's dramatic threads and romanticism lie the brutal realities of Southern life, through the representation of many slaves, but in particular Mammy, played by Hattie McDaniel. She's a fine addition to the cast, offering a caring maternal presence that could have instead been framed as simple comic relief—and McDaniel was the very first Black actor to win an Academy Award.

But there's one thing the film never openly acknowledges:

Mammy is a slave. This conflicts with how she's portrayed, as she lives with Scarlett O'Hara's family seemingly of her own volition, and there isn't reference to the fact that this is a character in forced servitude. Then there's the issue of the performance itself. While acted with integrity, the character can also at times seem like a walking minstrel show, speaking with the kind of broken English that would feel right at home in the work of the earlier director D. W. Griffith, who will be duly addressed in short order. If the film confronted and dissected the complexities of racism, Mammy's portrayal might be beneficial. But her role as a slave is completely glossed over in favor of the nearly four hours of drama—it's not quite glorified but not depicted with anywhere near the harsh reality slaves in her position and time were subjected to. As much as Quentin Tarantino's slavery-revenge epic *Django Unchained* (2012) sparked controversy for slavery's depiction in a borderline comedic context, compared to *Gone with the Wind*, it at least had the transparency to show the cruel horrors that Black people faced on a daily basis. A product of its time, *Gone with the Wind* failed to depict Mammy beyond the Southern gaze and imbue her with dignity and respect.

Another of the more egregious examples: *Breakfast at Tiffany's* (1961). As a whole, the film is a wonderful work. Inspired by Truman Capote's 1958 novella of the same name, the film perfectly translates if not the precise details of the story (the ending is given the classic kissing-in-the-rain Hollywood ending, a far cry from the bittersweetness of the source novel), then the distinctive sense of soapy, lace-curtain cattiness and bourgeoisie that the writer embodied both in his fictional voice and in the public eye.

Audrey Hepburn is beautiful and commanding in a rapid-fire,

dialogue-heavy role that could have easily fallen flat, and the story is a compelling one, tracing lost souls through a world of class and affluence not meant for people like them. Capote himself was less than enthusiastic about Hepburn's casting—he wanted Marilyn Monroe in the role of Holly Golightly and later remarked, "Paramount double-crossed me in every conceivable way and cast Audrey,"[103] though the film was a runaway success.

But looming over the Hollywood gloss is the racist specter of Mr. Yunioshi, Holly Golightly's cantankerous Japanese landlord, portrayed by Mickey Rooney. From the moment he's on-screen, the character is handled about as gracefully as a back-alley dog-fight, as if somewhere behind the scenes, a cash gamble was made that Rooney wouldn't dare make his portrayal offensive enough. The character is squinty-eyed, bucktoothed (thanks to some rather crude false teeth and facial prosthetics), and utterly buffoonish. He bangs his head against ceilings, runs into doorways, mugs for the camera, screams with a revving intensity, and speaks with a cringeworthy L-for-R accent that makes Ted Danson's 1993 blackface roast of Whoopi Goldberg look like an episode of *Blue's Clues*.

Mr. Yunioshi is more of a walking sight gag than an actual character. Why not give more flesh to his dramatic bones? It's not as if strict faithfulness to the source material was an ambition of the filmmakers, so that can't be it.

One of the film's producers, Richard Shepard, revealed in a DVD commentary for the film that he was trepid over the casting of Rooney, feeling that the role should go to someone of Japanese heritage.[104] But Blake Edwards, the director, wouldn't have it, keeping Rooney in the part for comedic value; apparently he felt that offending people wasn't a reason to limit what he saw as creative expression. Rooney himself claimed that for more than four decades following the film's release, he hadn't heard a word of the controversy, even incorporating clips of his performance in a one-man show he toured until his death. But when it was pointed out to him how many Japanese Americans found his portrayal insensitive, he also admitted to being heartbroken, saying that if he had known people would be offended, he "wouldn't have done it."[105]

The Council of Asian Pacific Islanders Together for Advocacy and Leadership addressed the controversy publicly in 2008, accusing the film of propagating "offensive, derogatory and hateful racial stereotypes detrimental and destructive to our society."[106] Shortly after the theater was contacted by the Council, it replaced a free Sacramento screening of *Breakfast at Tiffany's* with Pixar's *Ratatouille*; event planners decided it wasn't the most socially graceful film to show, especially in a year where race and change became a heated part of election-year conversation.

So why wasn't a Japanese actor cast in the role? The number of suitable actors was bountiful, even without the luxury of hindsight—imagine Toshiro Mifune, perhaps beneath some light age makeup, bringing Yunioshi to life in all his animated, dynamic intensity. Or perhaps another Akira Kurosawa regular, Takashi Shimura, bringing his grace and nobility to a role that was eventually flattened by its own tone-deaf ignorance. If the language barrier was an issue, an actor of Japanese descent may have somewhat redeemed the role.

As it is, the movie practically stops with a record-skipping screech whenever Yunioshi is on-screen. As a contemporary viewer, it's impossible to watch Rooney yukking it up without thinking, "Who in God's name actually thought this was a good idea?" Less than twenty years prior, Americans of Japanese heritage were separated from their fellow countrymen and forced to live in internment camps due to war-fueled xenophobia. Was the writing and casting of Yunioshi's character a reflection of persistent attitudes ingrained in the cultural psyche, an echo of hate rippling through the decades? Immortalized on the big screen at the expense of many.

Consider a film that was released only six years later with considerably more cultural sensitivity, albeit with flaws of its own: Stanley Kramer's *Guess Who's Coming to Dinner* (1967). Kramer's filmography isn't just infused with heightened social awareness; this awareness is one of his most essential creative pillars.

Consider *Judgment at Nuremberg* (1961), a scintillating and brilliantly acted portrayal of Nazi war crime and its aftermath that Kramer insisted on premiering in Berlin, and the controversial *Inherit the Wind* (1961), a courtroom procedural detailing the Scopes Monkey Trial, pitting evolution against creationism. Both films confront prickly issues with a steady camera and an even steadier mind, and both exist as cracking entertainment as well as a catalyst for long, introspective discussions. So it would make sense that in 1967, Kramer would turn his camera on racial tensions in America. At this time in history, America was experiencing particularly troublesome growing pains, as the youth of the 1950s embraced progressive ideals that clashed with the staunch customs of their parents and grandparents. Fade in on *Guess Who's Coming to Dinner.*

The story is relatively tame by contemporary standards but nonetheless a nail-biter for anybody with personal experience with rich, white America: a young woman named Joanna and a doctor named John Prentice return to San Francisco from Hawaii to meet Joanna's parents and announce their forthcoming marriage. The setup is rife with red flags—on the one hand, the two have known each other only for ten days, and they're already committing the rest of their lives to each other. Another alarm is that the parents weren't even aware of the relationship, let alone the marriage, ahead of time. Potentially even more controversially, which is exactly the point—Joanna is white and John is Black. And to make matters worse, they'll be in town for less than a day to explain the situation, giving Joanna's parents only a few hours to process the ordeal and its perceived consequences.

As the film begins, John is considerably more anxious than his idealist partner, who assures him that her parents are openly liberal and ready to embrace John as a new addition to their family. When the couple arrives, the situation that greets them is considerably less certain. Joanna's mother, played with an effortless intensity by the great Katharine Hepburn, trips over virtually every word she utters as she's confronted with the reality of Joanna and John's relationship. She claims to be progressive and not to be racist, but the film confronts that fact that this situation flies in the face of an entire lifetime's worth of social programming. The same is true of Joanna's father, who's even more alarmed by his daughter's relationship than his wife.

John immediately sees the trepidation behind the formalities and polite manners. So, without consulting Joanna, he gives her parents a one-sided ultimatum: he promises them he will marry their daughter only if there are absolutely no reservations about the matrimony from both mother and father. If there's even a slight snag, he'll break it off—he loves Joanna with all his heart, but he sees just how tight and essential her relationship to her parents is, and he couldn't bear to make her choose between her lover and her parents.

The film is a revelation for a number of reasons, some more obvious than others. On the surface, it's a film that punctuates racial tensions of its time. Interracial marriage was popular to talk about but not as popular to act on. While the film was in production in 1966, it was still illegal in sixteen states for people of different races to marry.[107] But in July 1967, while the film was still shooting, the Supreme Court's landmark decision in *Loving v. Virginia* struck down all state bans on interracial marriage as unconstitutional in one triumphant judicial wave.[108] It was the perfect timing, elevating the movie from activist think piece to an essential encapsulation of recent American progress.

But even more important than capturing the zeitgeist was the film's commentary on liberal America, its criticisms just as scathing as those attacking more conservative values. Joanna's father claims to be as liberal as can be, having put his weight as a major-league newspaper publisher behind many unspecified civil rights issues, yet when he's confronted with the reality of his daughter's relationship in his own home, a reality both he and his wife admit they had never even considered before, he's fundamentally uncomfortable. It might be easy to dismiss his anxieties as purely paternal—after all, beneath matters of racial difference, John and Joanna *are* announcing their marriage ten days after meeting, and such rushed news would strike any parent the wrong way. However, the film clearly reveals the insincerity behind a great deal of liberal lip service to progressive ideas. It's one thing to spout rhetoric—it's another to walk the walk as comfortably as you talk the talk.

Another key element of the film's substance is the way it flips the table. As the film goes on, John's parents agree to spontaneously fly from Los Angeles to San Francisco just to meet their son's bride-to-be, and they're unaware that she's white. John doesn't know how to break the news, and when his parents see Joanna for the first time, they are just as stunned as her parents—perhaps even more so. John's father voices his concerns right out of the gate and in even blunter terms than Joanna's father.

Resonating with moviegoers and critics alike, the film won screenwriter William Rose his only Academy Award and provided Hepburn a much-deserved win in the Best Actress category. *Guess Who's Coming to Dinner* even spawned a remake in 2005 titled *Guess Who*, with the racial tensions reversed—this time starring Bernie Mac as the father and Zoe Saldana taking home her white fiancé, played by Ashton Kutcher, to awkward effect. It's hardly the equal of Kramer's original—the writing isn't as sharp, and it relies on softer, more situational slapstick-inflected humor—but the leads charm in their roles, including Kutcher, who delivers one of his more endearing performances. The decision to shift the film away from the drama of the original and toward light comedy was one that Mac himself claimed reflected more open social attitudes. "Interracial dating is not that significant anymore," Mac said in a 2003 *USA Today* interview.[109] And he's right. The image of a Black woman with a white man may raise some eyebrows, but it no longer raises hell. And we may have the original film to thank for massaging images of mixed-race couples into mainstream entertainment, such as *Get Out (2017)* among others.

Any discussion of the history of Black representation in movies must include Spike Lee, perhaps the most important and outspoken director in this area. Trading time between small niche films and star-studded hits, Lee's filmmaking, highly stylized and unapologetically confrontational, has shed light on ways of life rarely explored in either mainstream or independent cinema: proud, richly depicted Black Americans living their daily lives in predominantly Black communities.

Sidney Poitier made films representing Black America, but he also had to work within a mainly non-Black system—nearly every mainstream movie about race before 1970 was assembled almost entirely by white people. Lee's films, on the other hand, are about Black people, by Black people and, at least partially, for Black people. Both in content and style, his films are as subtle as cannonballs to the kneecaps, but when compared to the calculated efforts of Hollywood's past, subtlety was a noxious gas to be burned away.

Spike Lee was born to a well-off family in Atlanta, Georgia, that made its way up the coast shortly after and settled in Brooklyn, New York. This would be Lee's stomping ground, the rich history and community eventually becoming a source of much of his filmmaking creativity. He attended New York University and made amateur, low-budget films through his twenties, culminating in his first mainstream success, *She's Gotta Have It*, in 1986. A shoestring indie film shot on 16mm black-and-white film featuring local actors and Spike Lee himself, the film was an exposé of the struggles of the modern Black woman, with skirt-chasing bachelors hounding her as she attempts to buck social expectations and live her life on her own terms. It's not quite polished—a rape scene near the end has aged particularly badly—and it may not get up in your face the way his later work does, but Lee's distinctive filmmaking style shines through the raggedy surface, and it established him as an important voice in independent cinema. The film also became one of the most financially successful movies of 1986 in terms of budget-to-profit ratio—made for only $175,000, its box-office gross was over $7 million, more than 40 times the investment.

Epitomizing both Lee's cinematic and political voices was the 1989 bombshell film *Do the Right Thing*. It was biting in its bluntness, capturing racial tensions in America in all their complexity. It begins as a slice-of-life mosaic of Black characters going through their daily motions in Brooklyn on the hottest day of summer and ends in a riotous climax that's as explosive and incendiary as it is troubling and intelligent.

The story is woven through the daily events in the life of Mookie, a young Black employee of a traditional Italian pizzeria in the heart of the neighborhood. The pizza shop is a hangout for much of the area's ethnically diverse youth, much to the discomfort of the Italian employees. They spit racist venom toward Mookie over the objections of Sal (played by Danny Aiello), the owner of the restaurant and a father figure for the employees. After slowly bringing things to a boil, the film reaches its crescendo after Giancarlo Esposito's character Buggin' Out is killed in a street confrontation, leading to protests, riots, and eventually the burning down of the pizzeria as an expression of deeply repressed Black anger at racial injustice.

That ending sparked one of the great controversies in late twentieth-century cinema, animating and, to the untrained eye, seemingly justifying suburban fears of urban uproar. The film is controversial by design, but only in the questions it asks. Lee leaves it to the audience to decide how right or wrong the ending is, though ultimately the answer doesn't matter: the point is tracing a continuity between racial discrimination and violent actions. It's not a lecture. It's a plea for understanding what it is like to be Black and a minority in America. *Do the Right Thing* produces some of the most memorable cinema of the past fifty years, inspiring empathy and humanity.

In 1991 and 1992 the world witnessed the videotaped beating of Black motorist Rodney King by Los Angeles police officers and the subsequent LA riots after the officers were acquitted—both events seemingly ripped straight from the script of Lee's film. But as any viewer from the Black community would tell you, that's hardly life imitating art: it only seemed that way to some after Lee had given light to the cycle of frustration and violence that plagues Black communities as a result of being disenfranchised and oppressed. As Martin Luther King Jr. put it, "It is a tortuous logic... to use the tragic results of segregation as an argument for the continuation of it."[110] Clearly a vicious cycle, still being unworked to this day.

D. W. Griffith

We can't ignore that filmmaking itself has fueled racism in America against Blacks. Spike Lee's vaccine was once the virus from host D. W. Griffith. This is the story of the origin of cinema and the most controversial movie ever made, *The Birth of a Nation* (1915).[111]

D. W. Griffith grew up in a small pocket of Kentucky in the late nineteenth century. His father, Jacob Griffith, had served as a Confederate officer in the American Civil War, and D. W. Griffith's early childhood was a picturesque portrait of Southern living. And as if to contrast the scope and expanse of his most ambitious works, his upbringing was also one of poverty, loss, and hardship. His father died when he was only ten years old, and later, his family struggling with financial disarray, Griffith dropped out of high school and spent his early adulthood working odd trade jobs. But for him, the gasp of air in the middle of all that difficulty was the world of theater. A local company, the Temple Theater, drew Griffith's attention during his employment as a bookstore clerk, and he quickly became acquainted with local actors, writers, and enthusiasts. The theater wasn't just an escape and an education—the theater was his world, and after years of supporting his family, he took a leap and joined a small troupe.

From here, Griffith jumped from company to company, city to city, honing his understanding of acting and branching out into playwriting and production. Though he saw little financial success from his select early plays, they allowed him to polish his storytelling instincts, eventually earning him a job in 1908 writing and acting for a New York–based studio called Biograph, one of the earliest movie studios in America. Within months he was granted the chance to shoot short projects, and he soon became the studio's main director. Over the next five years he made some four hundred short films for Biograph, eventually moving into features with *Judith of Bethulia* (1914), Biograph's first feature-length film. How strange to consider that more than a hundred years later, from the birth of film to the rise of digital technology, breaking into the industry works more or less the same way.

Griffith's career would deliver innovation in smooth, effective storytelling, with much of modern editing stemming from the sprawling narratives of his landmark works. *The Birth of a Nation* triumphs over them all, both in quality and in pure audacity—and in this instance, that is far from a compliment. Despite the film's acclaim as a technical marvel, and its wild box-office success, its handling of racism is nowhere near as graceful as its handling of narrative. From the very beginning, the Confederacy is depicted as a symbol of American idealism as the Civil War is mercilessly snuffed out.

The story is divided into two parts: pre-abolition and Reconstruction. One of the earliest title cards reads, "The bringing of the African to America planted the first seeds of disunion."[112] That sense of inhumanity stretches over the entire film, with Black people being either lampooned, targeted, or relegated to set decoration.

The film's first half follows the trials and tribulations of the Cameron family, wealthy plantation owners prospering in the boiling heat of South Carolina, and the Stoneman family, an abolitionist dynasty led by Austin Stoneman, a fictional analog for the real-life politician Thaddeus Stevens.

At the beginning of the film, the families are longtime friends—they frequently visit each other's homes, and the viewer senses in their interactions a familial bond that reaches beyond bloodlines. The screenplay follows these families as they adapt to the shifting landscape brought on by the Civil War and the liberation of slaves. Both families are torn apart by the war, with children thrown into the bloodbath of combat, and one family's faith in America is distorted into fear.

Ben Cameron, who would later become a colonel fighting for the Confederacy, develops a fixation from afar with Elsie Stoneman, played by silent-screen legend Lillian Gish. Until he arrives wounded at her infirmary, she has been oblivious to his existence. Contrary to the divide at its center, the Civil War actually brings these two star-crossed lovers together for the first time.

The Birth of a Nation's cast features a bizarre and stomach-churning mix of Black actors and white actors caked in blackface. To be Black performing next to a white man's most deplorable caricature of your race—nauseating. The film's closest attempt at a respectable Black character is Silas Lynch, a mixed-race right-hand man to Stoneman who is slimier than a salamander. He may be more educated and well spoken than the other Black characters, but that's where admiration ends.

In this film, Blacks come to embody the least attractive human traits Griffith can conjure: lazy, drunk, unintelligent, illiterate, conniving, predatory, and power hungry. Griffith seems to believe that's all there is to see in these characters. Even the most joyful scene, in which slaves to the Cameron family erupt into dance and laughter, is photographed with the distance you'd adopt for zoo animals, and we are invited to view them precisely that dismissively.

In this film, there is no hint of Blacks as disenfranchised minorities—in conjunction with the carpetbaggers, also seen as opportunistic, they are depicted as some kind of epidemic spreading across the land, overwhelming innocent white folks who are enduring their America being taken apart brick by brick after losing their honor in the war. Abraham Lincoln, whose physical portrayal is as spitting-image accurate as any film incarnation before or after, is cast as a bleeding heart and a pushover, a puppet for the Blacks and Yankees, and the other abolitionists are depicted as being driven by a desire for wealth and control.

One of various cringeworthy scenes: Black soldiers, portrayed by white actors in blackface, pass by Colonel Cameron with prideful spite after the confederates are defeated. Following behind is

Silas, who comments that the Carolina ground belongs to them just as much as anybody else, "'*Colonel*' Cameron." The emphasis is placed on his name for the purpose of posturing. What should be an expression of equality is used by the filmmakers to cast Blacks as braggadocious bullies flaunting their basic freedom over an innocent white couple in a broken country. From this moment, Colonel Cameron's journey continues to escalate—he witnesses the death of a dear friend after we see her chased by an insatiable Black man behaving as single-mindedly as a woodland predator. As Cameron holds her crumpled body in his arms, the hate begins to burn behind his eyes.

With a demon rigidly defined, emotions fuming as a result of the loss of the war, the plot turns to the birth of the Ku Klux Klan, who are painted not as a hate group exercising cruelty and terrorism to enforce regressive and reprehensible attitudes, but as a force of supreme dignity spreading across the South, coming to the Confederacy's defense, and bringing stability to territory infested with Northern scum. When Klan members don their white hoods for the first time, the musical score swells with triumphant, patriotic awe. As they ride through the dusty streets, fighting back against a borderline rabid Black horde, they're displayed as nothing short of venerable heroes.

At the time of the film's release in 1915, the influence of the Klan had been all but extinguished—contrary to Griffith's flattering depiction. They weren't the beacon of hope and change they purported to be, rather a fringe group that emerged from the ripples of the Civil War. But you couldn't tell that to the storm surrounding the film. White hoods, cloaks, and other iconography inspired by the film and the KKK were sold at movie theaters and elsewhere—some theater ushers even dressed in white robes while they admitted people in and out of their screenings.

Even stranger, the movie was the first ever presented at the White House, with President Woodrow Wilson—not exactly the most racially progressive politician—allegedly completely bowled over by its take on a decaying way of life. One of the more alarming legends haunting movie lore is the adoration the president had for the film—reportedly, Wilson said, "It is like writing history with lightning, and my only regret is that it is all so terribly true,"[113] though the historical legitimacy of this somewhat murky.[114] If that truly was how blind the president of the United States was to its blatant bigotry, imagine how the average citizen must have reacted to it.

But the match wouldn't truly be struck until a preacher named William Joseph Simmons discovered the film's existence and saw a nefarious opportunity. Simmons was bedridden from a car accident, which allowed him ample time to follow and obsess over the film's string of headlines. He saw the film as a platform to rebrand the KKK and return the organization, and indeed the organized world, to its former glory (if that's even an applicable word). More importantly, when he finally saw the film himself, he witnessed an image that he would catapult into popular culture: white robes gathering around a cross engulfed in flames of bigotry. Believe it or not, the image of a burning cross wasn't popularized until the debut of Griffith's epic. The practice existed for generations in Scotland, where clans would alert each other from afar with this signal. But it wasn't until Griffith's film that the practice became widely metastasized to radical people burning crosses dressed in white robes, an image Griffith derived from illustrations in Thomas Dixon Jr.'s 1905 novel *The Clansman: A Historical Romance of the Ku*

Klux Klan. For Simmons, race hatred was indeed a romance.

The man hatched a plan. A peaceful demonstration that sent just the right message. He reached out to two surviving members of the Klan's original iteration, gathered twelve others of similarly rotten spirit, and planned to climb Stone Mountain, plant a cross, and publicly burn it in conjunction with *The Birth of a Nation*'s winter release in Atlanta, Georgia. And that's what they did, on Thanksgiving night, 1915. The America they loved had seen enough progress for their taste, and it was time to speak their mind in grandiose fashion. The fifteen charter members declared the Klan born again, with Simmons naming himself the "Imperial Wizard."[115] Revived and rebranded, thanks to D. W. Griffith's *The Birth of a Nation*.

Soon burning crosses and white robes became synonymous with the KKK, and sadly, these images inspired many. Despite its racism, the film is considered one of the greatest box-office successes of all time, ranking only behind *Titanic* and *Avatar* when the gross receipts are adjusted for inflation.[116] In fact, the film was successful enough to produce the very first sequel film ever made, *The Fall of a Nation* (1916), directed by Thomas Dixon Jr., author of the original book. The middling group of KKK members assembled by Simmons soon ballooned into tens of thousands, then hundreds of thousands, and then millions.

This kind of power and influence is exactly what makes the film's objective quality so troubling. It isn't just a good yarn—it's a masterpiece of cinematic construction before the word *masterpiece* lost its luster. In the movies of D. W. Griffith, one can feel cinema itself being born in subtle camera moves and groundbreaking editing. They are as important to the evolution of storytelling as crystallized cave paintings of hunters and roaming buffalo. That movies over a hundred years old, so far removed from contemporary cinematic language, can still hold up as compelling stories is nothing short of a miracle. *The Birth of a Nation* weaves its narrative carefully and meticulously over the course of its 190 minutes, with Griffith and company exercising their command fearlessly and with utmost focus, delivering scenes of the Civil War so graceful in their framing, one can see the ingredients of virtually every subsequent war film blooming all at once in single moments. There is one shot in particular in which we fade in on a woman, apparently Native American, embracing two terrified children before the camera pans away from them, hiding them from a slowly revealed battlefield crawling with soldiers picking each other off like hunting trophies. This single movement expresses more about the scope of war than a dozen histrionic speeches.

Precisely because of its skillful assembly, *The Birth of a Nation*'s impact is devastating. The push and pull of the romance is genuinely compelling, and the dissolution of a multigenerational friendship proves gradually heartbreaking. One truly feels the weight of history being channeled through the prisms of these two patriarchal families.

If we view these satisfying narrative elements through the lens of Bandura's theory of behavioral modeling, however, the audience is encouraged to identify with negative behaviors—the white men are presented as being positive, just, and victimized.[117] From the movie's perspective, the negative models aren't the racists representing regressive ideals, but the Black people, portrayed as thwarting the ambition that fuels the American dream, a dream the film argues is dying every day.

But fear not, anxious readers, for the film garnered just as many critics as it did admirers. Activist initiatives protested the movie nationwide, and many cities censored it emphatically. It's still widely considered one of the most racist mainstream films ever made. Various civil rights groups condemned the film as having a hideously skewed perspective on history, glorifying attitudes and individuals unfit for the silver screen.

Is it at all possible that Griffith didn't grasp the full implications of the film he was making? Did he not fully understand the power of story? We might speculate that his core intention wasn't to alienate Black people and revitalize the KKK to a new national force but rather to craft a eulogy to the same Southern values his father seemed to represent—his father who fought for the Confederacy. If that was the case, he made the fatal mistake of not seeing the forest for the trees. His ode to traditional views turned into a literal witch hunt—of an already hugely oppressed demographic. Yet, this is a theory that lets Griffith off easy, and his next move should be an important consideration here.

Griffith was so disturbed by the sensationalism surrounding his film that he couldn't sit quietly. It was one thing to disagree with the content of his art; he felt that attempts to censor it across the country sullied the act of making art in the first place. Art is a statement, and if you can't speak freely regardless of the opinions of others, he argued, how are we doing justice to the American way? Thus he began work on his next film, *Intolerance* (1916), another sprawling three-hour epic intended as a response to this harsh criticism and censorship. In short, he didn't pause to reflect; he ardently doubled down.

Both in plot and technical scope, *Intolerance* was an even

bigger undertaking than *The Birth of a Nation*, combining four different narrative stretches set in different time periods: a thread set in Babylon chronicling the historic fall of the city; one following the pressure that built up to the St. Bartholomew's Day Massacre of 1572; a more contemporary story in which a young man (played by Robert Harron) and woman (played by Mae Marsh) struggle to survive in a world that grows more money obsessed by the day; and a sequence depicting the events that crescendoed into nothing less than the crucifixion of Jesus. All of these narrative threads are linked by intolerance—the refusal to listen to each other and treat each other fairly. They begin building on one another, picking up speed slowly, then not so slowly, until all four stories reach their climax at the same time, resulting in one of the earliest triumphs of narrative momentum that wouldn't be outclassed until perhaps *Battleship Potemkin* (1925).

In 2016, a film directed by Nate Parker about the life of slave rebellion leader Nat Turner was also titled *The Birth of a Nation* in an attempt to take control of the name and rebrand it into the context of Black empowerment. The great irony is that Parker's film became embroiled in a controversy of its very own surrounding the filmmaker's alleged past, which meant that despite being the largest purchase ever of a single film at the Sundance Film Festival at $17.5 million, it lost virtually all of its award-season potential and ultimately floundered at the mainstream box office.

Griffith's own life ended on a similarly defeated note. Though he maintained positive relationships with his collaborators, his films began to lose money, and by 1924 he was forced out of United Artists, the movie studio he had cofounded in 1919. He gave up directing after the box-office failure of his film *The Struggle*

(1931)—an unfortunately apt title—although he never formally quit, continuing to produce and assist in the technical achievements of other people's films until his death in 1948.

The story of Griffith and his late-career fizzle raises a very important question: to what extent is the filmmaker responsible for the potential impact of the content he or she produces? It's been a debate that has raged virtually as long as the existence of art itself. On one side of the scale, you have the idea that the expression itself is the end of the artist's responsibility to the world. That's a very attractive idea for obvious reasons. For starters, it essentially removes the ceiling often felt by artists as they attempt to reconcile their imagination with public expectations. It also encourages personal responsibility, or what many commonly refer to today as media literacy, within the audiences that consume art.

Stanley Kubrick was a controversial figure on numerous fronts, but a single act of restraint, humility, and decency draws a very defined line in the sand between him and Griffith: response to controversy. And in a strangely ironic twist, it was his most scandalous achievement that provided his opportunity for redemption.

A Clockwork Orange, a polarizing tale of mayhem and morality based on an even more provocative and controversial book, lit the world ablaze—often at its own expense—when it hit theaters in 1971. The media condemned the film as tasteless and exploitative of violence and depravity, with even Roger Ebert famously giving the film a condemnatory two-star review, referring to the movie's depiction of unchained violence as "an ideological mess."[118] Yet it's also a masterpiece. The moral muddle is part of the film's timeless power, with a story so compelling and well calibrated, you almost don't realize that you're being persuaded into empathizing with a main character who's essentially an unrepentant psychopath in a two-hour dissection of ethics.

To the horror of a nation, that empathy tipped over into emulation, with deadly results. In the months following the UK release of the film there were reports of copycat crimes, people forming gangs, prowling the streets with mischievous intent, and even wearing the same costumes as Kubrick's delinquent on-screen characters. That these were hardly innocent pretenders was signified by several acts of violence: a homeless man was bludgeoned to death for what amounted to pocket change,[119] just like the scene that plays out early in the film ("Can you spare some cutter, me brothers?"); and, in another horrifying case a seventeen-year-old girl from the Netherlands was attacked and raped by a group of men at night in a crime chillingly evocative of the film's initial home-invasion scene: Malcolm McDowell's Alex DeLarge croons "Singin' in the Rain" during an identical act of sexual assault.[120]

In an unprecedented move, Stanley Kubrick, previously a staunch opponent of the linking of art with real-world violence, struck a deal with Warner Brothers that pulled the film from every British cinema. The film wasn't simply censured; the United Kingdom attempted to scrub every atom of the film's existence from public access, a movement led by the director himself in a bizarre and perhaps existential crisis of awakening to his very own cinematic impact. And for nearly thirty years, the campaign was successful. According to the *Guardian*'s Peter Bradshaw, even ordering an imported DVD for private use was prohibited, as customs would seize copies of the film to prevent distribution of any kind.[121] It wasn't until shortly after Kubrick's death in 1999 that the ban was finally lifted.

It's not entirely clear what the motivation was behind Kubrick's change of heart—some reports claim it was due to threats against the lives of him and his family. But the point is that action was taken, however drastic, in response to the overpowering nature of the work he had created.

Compare that action to that of D. W. Griffith. While Kubrick did what he felt was the responsible thing when confronted with the reality of his impact, regardless of personal philosophy, D. W. Griffith didn't simply double down—he made an hours-long epic that was, at least in his mind, a case for his own victimhood and righteousness. Did D. W. Griffith collapse professionally by falling on his own sword?

Despite moral judgment, the pictures admittedly live on, and in that sense, so does Griffith in all his complexity. His legacy is not purely the racism of *The Birth of a Nation* or the retaliation of *Intolerance*—he is remembered more broadly as a true innovator and pioneer in what cinema can do. Yet outside the artistry of filmmaking, that facility carries over into moving images' effect on reality. Life imitating art. For good. And in this case, bad. What happens when this propensity is exploited and militarized for even more perverse ends?

Leni Riefenstahl

The word *propaganda* has always had a dirty connotation. Just hearing the word is almost enough to dismiss whatever idea it's attached to. Many filmmakers, including the likes of John Huston, Frank Capra, and Sergei Eisenstein, have indulged in the making of films purely to raise national morale. None, however, have reached the trendsetting heights of Leni Riefenstahl.

Her filmography is as controversial as *The Birth of a Nation*, yet her techniques were as influential to the evolution of film language as those of Alfred Hitchcock and Orson Welles. Of all the women in film, from editor Margaret Booth to writer and director Penny Marshall, Riefenstahl is perhaps the most famous woman to ever step behind the camera, and her shadow continues to stretch over cinema to this day.

Every film student remembers the moment from *Triumph of the Will* (1935), Riefenstahl's worryingly powerful Nazi propaganda film, in which high divers mid-fall are seen soaring, as if turning the air itself into a cinematic ocean. What about the moment in *Olympia* (1938), her flawlessly kinetic account of Olympic competition, in which we see a hurled disc stretching against a cloudy sky, one of the most dynamic images in all of documentary film? This kind of innovation was her bread and butter, as if her foremost agenda was not just to sway opinion but rather to sway it in new, never-before-seen ways. It's part of what makes her legacy such a dangerous one.

What value is genius, however titanic, if it's used to persuade people in favor of fascist dictatorships or poisonous ideologies? Is breaking new ground enough to justify clouding the truth? Perhaps it's not best we start there. To understand Leni Riefenstahl's art, we must first understand who she was and how she came to be the preternatural talent that produced such a troubling history.

Riefenstahl was born in August 1902 in Germany, and her father, a plumber, raised her in a rather domineering fashion that only fueled her lifelong rebellious streak. Proudly strong-willed and independent-minded, she didn't subscribe to the more subservient inflections of the gender roles of her era, and her mother, a seamstress, encouraged her iconoclasm. Her father, though, tried to quash this free spirit. When Riefenstahl developed an interest in dance—an interest that would inadvertently alter the course of her life—he did not approve, and when he discovered she had been taking lessons behind his back, he shipped her away to boarding school to be broken down into a more disciplined, obedient creature. The conceit is, in retrospect, laughable. It's not likely that her father was a very smart man, because one of the core aspects of the school's curriculum was, in fact, theater and dance. Far from diminishing her drive, Riefenstahl's time at boarding school proved formative, and her time away from family cultivated the qualities that would make her a trailblazer of unflappable spirit.

Like the birth of cinema itself with the early works of the Lumière brothers, for young Leni Riefenstahl, it all began with a train. Waiting impatiently at Nollendorfplatz station to visit a doctor to assess a serious dancing injury, she saw a poster for the 1924 film *Mountain of Destiny*. The poster's image, a striking black-and-white figure leaping from one side of a rocky chasm to another, shook Riefenstahl so completely to her core that from that moment on, she knew cinema would become one of her greatest loves.

Riefenstahl went immediately to the cinema advertised on the poster and saw the film directed by Arnold Fanck, a geologist with aspirations to immortalize precious rock faces. This was more than the carnival attraction the early innovators of cinema had made—it was an immersive experience that used its techniques to tell a compelling story of father-to-son generational triumph.

Lead actor Luis Trenker gracefully played a character trying to climb the same mountain that had killed his father. Never one to pass up an opportunity, Riefenstahl reached out to Trenker to express an interest in being his co-lead in the next film by Arnold Fanck. Trenker passed the message on to Fanck along with a photograph of the young Riefenstahl. Her ethereal beauty won over both figures in spite of their initial skepticism, and Fanck saw a star in the making. In fact, Fanck asked Riefenstahl to play not the co-lead but the leading role. Their first film together was *The Holy Mountain* (1926), a montage of harsh imagery and frostbitten cinematography.

Riefenstahl would continue to collaborate with Fanck and even work with acclaimed filmmaker G. W. Pabst on one project, all the while sponging up the craft of filmmaking in all its details and techniques. These experiences were, in their red-cheeked, ice-cold rigor, the best film school one could ever ask for—imagine learning not just from the master of cinema but from some of the people who developed its very language in the first place.

These experiences motivated Riefenstahl to produce, direct, and star in the first film of her own authorship: 1932's *The Blue Light*. A kind of expressionist fantasy with realistic edges, the film follows Junta, a free-spirited girl ostracized by her village on suspicion of being a witch. Riefenstahl was as exacting in the making of the film as her teacher Arnold Fanck, unbending in her demands on both crew and studio. It took unparalleled gusto, perhaps even arrogance, to demand not only the construction of special lenses by American designers but also the creation of a special film stock to help her shoot nighttime scenes more convincingly. But she did it, and in the end, she got her way in both cases. She even cast aside the commonplace practice of building sets at a studio lot, making her film one of the very first to be shot entirely on location—in real houses, in real churches.

All the while, the first inklings of the Nazi Party were nipping at Germany's heels. Riefenstahl was persuaded by one of her collaborators to attend a Nazi rally in Berlin at which Adolf Hitler would be speaking. She at first refused, but she caved at the insistence that it might change her life. And it did. She was enraptured by Hitler, swept up in his impassioned rhetoric and his effortless appeal as a leader. She was so compelled by his speaking, in fact, that she wrote him a letter, and to her surprise, he wrote her a response, citing that he not only knew of her but was very fond of her films, especially one scene from *The Sacred Mountain* in which her silhouette dances by a yellow-tinted sea. She was charmed by his contrasting character traits, fiery and convincing before a fawning crowd but friendly and personable during more intimate exchanges. She sensed in him a dangerous man but also one who might be able to steer an ailing Germany back onto the road to glory. In the same way Riefenstahl was entranced by his charisma, Hitler was entranced by her fearlessness and mastery of filmmaking. He invited her to start making films for his party when they rose to power, but Riefenstahl waved away the offer, not taking it seriously in the slightest.

Eventually, though, Hitler's command and showmanship turned her into putty in his hands. When he was finally in power, she did ultimately produce a propaganda film for the Nazi Party, and like *The Birth of a Nation*, it became one of the most masterful executions of moral bankruptcy existing in the firmament of film. *Triumph of the Will* is perhaps the greatest known propaganda film of all time, more so even than Eisenstein's 1925 Soviet film *Battleship Potemkin*. Say what you will about *Potemkin*'s biases—it's a straightforward story of heroism that laid the groundwork of cinema. So, too, did *Triumph of the Will*, arguably the very peak of Riefenstahl's technical prowess, lending some of the most uniquely possessing imagery of the early twentieth century to shamelessly glorifying the Nazis to the likes of gods.

The film's very first image depicts the Nazis' most imposing symbol, a robust statue of an eagle poised for glory, as the musical score begins to swell. When defending the piece as a work of art, Riefenstahl claimed there were no depictions of the Nazis doing anything particularly suspect—and she was right. There are no raids of Jewish neighborhoods, no gas chambers, no furnaces. And although the reverence for Nazi symbolism is on unapologetic display, there aren't any explicitly anti-Semitic references in the film. And that's precisely the problem. The Nazis are displayed in the midst of a kind of political ballet, every last soldier framed with ceremonial dignity. Hitler himself is framed in a particularly fawning way, placed in one scene against a cloudy sky from an extremely low angle, communicating the almost cosmic authority he exuded before audiences.

In one of the film's most notable camera moves, the dolly tracks in a circle around Hitler as he speaks, as if hanging on to the edge of his every word. Similarly, throughout the film Hitler is always shot from below and never shares the frame with anyone. The intended effect is clear—to induce awe and reverence of Hitler and to present him as larger than life.

Beneath the queasy feeling that the viewer is complicit in an act of historical injustice, the film is beautiful to watch. That's what made it such effective propaganda. Every shot pours faultlessly into the next like water off a rock face, the whole film assembled without the slightest interruption of flow or momentum.

Did Riefenstahl understand the ideas of the empire she would elevate through her work? Or was she simply one of many pawns Hitler seduced with his rhetoric? While Hitler rose to power, Riefenstahl was at times off filming in the mountains, which usually coincided with key moments of the Third Reich's political unrest. Whenever Riefenstahl spoke to Hitler about the troubling things said about him, he deflected and dissuaded, creating an air of secrecy around his true intentions.

It's hard to know what lay beneath Riefenstahl's decision to go ahead and make her first film for the Nazi Party, but according to her, it was just a footnote in her oeuvre and not even a film—rather a scant collection of shots of a party address that was ruined by interruptions during shooting. Riefenstahl downplaying her film's intentions, design, and impact this way does sound like revisionist history. The techniques she invented and utilized to present Hitler as godlike speak for themselves.

As in the work of D. W. Griffith, the most frightening thing about Riefenstahl's filmography is the blending of technical innovation with sordid ends. After *Triumph of the Will* came the 1938 documentary *Olympia*. From the very first frames, the film is an experiment in pushing the boundaries of cinematographic conventions. Though its narrative is relatively ambient, the camera keeps gliding with zero friction throughout the work as an ode to Olympic athletes, particularly German ones, as the most heroic in the world.

Riefenstahl's film is constantly in motion. Even when she holds the camera still, whether on an excited spectator, a referee, or a five-star pole vaulter preparing for launch, something in frame is bringing the film to vivid life. From the moment the activities begin, you're not just in the stands—you're on the field, you're above the world, you're next to people flexing their muscular and spiritual core.

Riefenstahl didn't make a film *about* the Olympics as much as she made one *from* them. No talking heads. No pedantic narration. Just a historic event given permission to play out as it happened, guided only by her unrivaled attention to detail. But don't let the lack of agenda fool you—there's still a narrative being built shot for shot, subject by subject, and a point of view that's unmistakable: an almost fetishistic tribute to superior fitness and an admiration for striving and peak human excellence. In light of her politically questionable filmography, some critics have interpreted this call to excellence as fascist in nature, but Riefenstahl once again refuted that notion, claiming there was no inherent connection between art and politics, and aesthetics was her sole agenda in shooting the landmark film.

These films were acclaimed across Europe after premiering in Berlin to rapturous warmth. But when Riefenstahl brought the films to America, the reception was far less welcoming, far more hostile—in the eyes of Hollywood, Riefenstahl had become the cinematic voice of the Nazi Party, and no work of art could eclipse that fact. While Riefenstahl was journeying across the world and presenting her art, the Third Reich had begun its full-fledged extermination of not only Jewish lives but all cultural artifacts bearing their signature. Artwork created by Jews, houses, temples, whole towns were vandalized or destroyed.

When questioned about her knowledge of the Nazis' activity, Riefenstahl claimed total ignorance, at first accusing people of lying and spreading rumors. But gradually, as the news of Nazi atrocities hit more and more newspaper covers, the reality dawned on her—she hadn't had anywhere near a complete grasp on the powers with whom she had unwittingly allied. Or, at least that's what she insisted on in subsequent interviews.

The evidence to the contrary came in the form of the production of what would be her last film for forty-eight years, *Tiefland*, a fiction film shot from 1940 to 1944 but not completed and released until 1954. It would see Riefenstahl finally return to acting after years of being swept up in the world of documentaries. Following in the visually adventurous tradition of her previous work while remaining slightly more narratively conventional—a bit too much so for some critics at the time—the film itself would have been largely innocuous had it not been for a crucial and ultimately horrifying creative choice: a scene for which Riefenstahl had workers from concentration camps shipped to the set to be used as extras.

Such a revelation seems to fly completely in the face of Riefenstahl's claims to ignorance. As the harrowing documentary *A Film Unfinished* demonstrated in 2010, it's well known that propaganda films and newsreels warped reality in favor of the Nazis, depicting concentration camps as perfectly civil and comfortable environments for all kinds and ages, almost like halfway homes where Jews and others were provided with food, water, and shelter, and most people on-screen were far cries from the skeletal and abused bodies we now know were almost universally present in the camps. Even so, it seems inconceivable that Riefenstahl wouldn't know the truth.

Riefenstahl's involvement with the Nazis cost her the rest of her filmmaking career and in many ways left an unhealable scar across her entire life. Once the war officially ended, during a process referred to as the denazification trials, all individuals involved with or possessing connections to the Third Reich were rounded up and tried for war crimes, and that included Leni Riefenstahl. Though it was now openly known that Riefenstahl had spent personal time with Hitler on numerous occasions, it was judged that she could not be labeled a war criminal due to her lack of overtly political involvement with the party. Instead, she wore the crown of Nazi sympathizer until the day she died, forcing her into relative reclusion from her fellow Germans for decades.

But her condemnation in the public consciousness didn't stop her from pursuing further artistic goals. She remained active as a photographer and filmmaker, although she released only photos, never finishing or releasing the work she did in film. Her most famous work from this period is a book of photographs of the societally isolated culture of the Nuba people of Sudan. These bold, honest photos contain all the power of her film work without the tinge of her wartime involvements and connections. There's a melancholic poetry to the time she spent with the Nuba people, having nested with them for eight months to more deeply document their culture and daily lives. Though she recorded countless hours of footage, she never released any of it to the public or assembled it into any satisfying end. Here was a group of people that saw her only as Riefenstahl, having absolutely no knowledge of the World War or the atrocities of the Nazi Party she had glorified and helped bring to power through film.

To the world of cinema, Leni Riefenstahl existed practically as a memory even as she remained alive, having no engagement with the film community through exhibition of her work, leading many to think she'd retired for good. But this was the same person who as a young woman had so fearlessly climbed mountains on film, and retreat was not in her tradition—no matter how tired or beaten, a woman of her stature and talent owed herself one last gasp. In 2002, just a few days before her hundredth birthday, Leni Riefenstahl released her final film, her first finished project in nearly fifty years: an oceanographic documentary titled *Impressionen Unter Wasser* (*Impressions of the Deep*). Though hardly a revolutionary leap belonging in the pantheon of her classics—the film was shot on video in grainy digitized color—some of the world nonetheless welcomed her return, her trespasses forgiven. It had been far too long, and unfortunately, her death the following year only served to punctuate that fact. Her disappearance left the impact of a sequoia crashing to the forest floor after years of looming large—at 101 years old, the loss of Leni Riefenstahl felt like committing a piece of the birth of cinema to graceful rest.

But her legacy will never be at rest, and neither should our analysis of it. What can we as storytellers learn from her rose-tinted depiction of the Nazi Party? It's certainly complicated. She eventually denounced Hitler and the Third Reich when denial was no longer possible. But up until her death, she denied too that *Triumph of the Will* did any kind of glorifying, noting that she had only wanted to make an interesting film as a piece of art rather than milquetoast newsreel, and that people who wrote such antagonistic things about her were stupid and didn't understand her work. Her attitude toward her films is troubling in the same way as D. W. Griffith's; he also dismissed the criticism of his films and their perceived political criminality. If there's any question to ask yourself, it's this: if you had been present at Riefenstahl's trial during denazification, if you had heard her arguments side by side with the evidence of the documentary itself and the damage its exalted political empire swept across all of Europe, would you deem her a war criminal?

While Riefenstahl was pardoned judicially, the public saw the writing on the wall, and she was ostracized socially. As Werner Herzog once said, "The poet must not avert his eyes"—but a poet speaks from the heart, and arguably, so did Riefenstahl to her detriment when she used her lens to orchestrate propaganda for one of the most heinous mass murderers in human history.

Frank Capra

Old-fashioned. Two words that can be laudatory or condemnatory depending on the connotation. And when you think of such films, you think of films with soaring love stories, saccharine scores. There are filmmakers who decry so-called message films as pat, unambiguous, and therefore unchallenging to audiences and unfulfilling to create. But for every rule, there's an exception, and Frank Capra was an exception in virtually every creative decision he made. Frank Capra was old-fashioned. He was also a genius at creative populist entertainment that sold subversive ideas to a public that might not otherwise be open to them.

But as we transition from Leni Riefenstahl, a propagandist, to Frank Capra, the man with a message, it's important to outline the distinction between the two approaches. Perhaps as you've been reading this book, the discomfiting aspects of social engineering—which can be used for manipulative and predatory ends—have crept into your psyche, and here is a good opportunity to clear the air. The difference between propaganda and message storytelling is that propaganda doesn't concern itself with dialectic but rather the bombardment and unflinching continuation of an idea. *Hitler is godlike and the Nazi Party is supreme*, as is depicted in *Triumph of the Will*, for example, versus *how do we as mothers and fathers continue to support our children in this changing culture of interracial marriage* in *Guess Who's Coming to Dinner?* The contrast is the existence of debate, the openness to perspective and facts, and—paramount—that the dialectic engages rather than subverts critical reason in its viewers. Message films argue the point carefully from one sound premise to the next, while propaganda uses tactics of manipulation to get audiences to swallow the pill whole. As long as you're putting your central idea on trial, rather than dismissing all opposing points of view, it's a step in the right direction. If you're stacking the deck in favor of your message, you're cheating your audience. If you're stacking the deck against your message, you're challenging them and ultimately hitting deeper truths.

Now that the air is a bit fresher, let's return to Frank Capra's Herculean career. Born in 1897, Capra was raised by working-class Sicilian parents on Italian soil and didn't come to the United States until he was six years old. With a childhood mimicking the spirit of the-people-against-the-odds that would define his storytelling, he checks virtually every box for the template of the American success story.

From his very first moments, Capra struggled. He was born a sickly child and wasn't expected to live. He worked a multitude of jobs from an early age: he was everything from a technician at the Western Pipe and Steel plant to a janitor boy, and he even played guitar on weekend nights when he wasn't busy stuffing papers for the *Los Angeles Times*.[122] Somehow, through the power of his tireless work ethic, he was able to chip in toward his family's well-being while also being a prodigious high school student, graduating Manual Arts High School at the age of 17. His childhood companions suggested that while he didn't avoid anyone, he was rarely available to play with other kids; he was studying and making money.

When he finally started college at the Throop Polytechnic Institute (now California Institute of Technology), Capra continued to work while attending school, including one position assisting engineers at the Pasadena Light and Power plant. Capra was always focused on getting the job done, ready and willing to get his hands dirty if needed. This would prove essential to execute the kind of tightly calibrated personal vision he would become known for as a filmmaker. But rather surprisingly, Capra didn't attend school for training in movies—such a thing didn't really exist in the early twentieth century. Instead, Capra majored in chemical engineering in hopes of making it a profession.

As his university days drew to a close, Capra was preparing to uproot, enlisting in the Army in 1917 to serve his country in World War I. After graduating in 1918, he was stationed at the Presidio in San Francisco, where he taught writing and mathematics to other soldiers for two months before being discharged on account of a nasty bout of Spanish flu.[123] This began something of a transitional period for the director: after his military service ended, he returned to what he knew best: labor, performing various odd jobs to "get the moolah," eventually developing poker-playing skills with which he would earn a rather significant portion of his living.

While supplementing his jobs by peddling reading materials door-to-door, Capra spotted an advertisement in one of the books about a new studio opening in San Francisco. He subsequently talked his way into the role of property man, splicer, title designer, assistant director, and director.

For the purpose of brevity, we'll cover only a small portion of Capra's filmography here, as aside from being a master populist, he was a surprisingly prolific artist for someone of such consistent quality. Some films are, nonetheless, better than others, punctuating the thesis of Capra's cinematic legacy: the man against the world. Throughout his five decades of working in the film industry, Capra compiled a portfolio of nearly fifty movies—with a whopping five of them deemed historically significant and preserved in the National Film Registry. Much like Rainer Werner Fassbinder and Sidney Lumet, he made more great movies than most directors have made movies. But Capra's streak of slyly political, liberal films wouldn't begin until he'd earned a certain amount of autonomy within the industry with his runaway hit *It Happened One Night* (1934).

In Frank Capra's first true bona fide hit, the sentimental director would marry the on-screen talents of leading man du jour Clark Gable and leading lady Claudette Colbert. The two weave a romantic comedy based on the age-old law that opposites attract with stellar intensity, producing laughs and tears in a film that might on its surface appear to be something of an uncharacteristic piece for Capra. It features social undertones for those who choose to dig them out, but they're buried in a story whose primary agenda is to charm and entertain.

Capra partnered on *It Happened One Night* with producer Harry Cohn, who headed Columbia Pictures. He adapted the premise of the short story "Night Bus" by Samuel Hopkins Adams. The film centers around Ellie Andrews (Claudette Colbert), who grows up rich and elopes with pilot King Westley, of whom her father,

Alexander Andrews (Walter Connolly), is not fond. Alexander—the not so great, in Ellie's eyes—goes to great lengths to end the marriage because he believes King Westley is in it only for the money. Upset, Ellie runs away in hopes of reuniting with her lover. As she boards a bus, she meets a recently out-of-work reporter, Peter Warne (Clark Gable). Peter says that if she gives him an exclusive on her love-bound story, he will help her reunite with King. If she refuses, he will tell her father of her whereabouts. Ellie complies. This leads to Peter and Ellie traveling around together and, take a guess, falling in love. In the meantime, Alexander has offered a reward of $10,000 for anyone who finds Ellie.

Toward the end of their travels, Ellie notices Peter is gone from their motel, and she assumes he has abandoned her. She calls Alexander, rushes home, and agrees to properly marry King upon hearing that her dad and the pilot have made amends. But Peter wasn't leaving Ellie—he was off selling a newspaper story about their plan to wed, so he could have a few dollars in his pocket for their nuptials.

Now with love lost, Ellie reveals to her father all that has transpired. Alexander admits to receiving a wire from Peter, requesting a meeting in regards to a financial matter. Ellie is disgusted, and the wedding with King is given the go-ahead.

Traveling to meet Alexander, Peter demands payment for all Ellie put him through: $39.60. On principle he refuses the hefty $10,000 award previously offered, taking only the reimbursement of expenses from their trip. Alexander shares this with his daughter, after readying her getaway vehicle, paving the way for Ellie to dump King at the altar.

This simple plot stole every single major prize at the Academy

Awards the following year. But what was so spectacular about this story? Capra's *It Happened One Night* gave the audience a chance to, in this instance, *feel* better.

The movie launched right in the middle of the Great Depression. Economic collapse plagued the entire nation, with everybody from working-class families to formerly successful entrepreneurs finding themselves in publicly funded soup lines just to stay alive. Here was a movie that was a slate wiped clean of propaganda and wartime tensions, providing a cathartic escape from day-to-day survival of the Depression. *Variety* magazine said the film was "without a particularly strong plot [but] manages to come through in a big way, due to the acting, dialog, situations and direction."[124]

Claudette Colbert, the female lead, expressly stated that she hated working on set and hated the movie. Turns out Capra was not the biggest fan of her, either. He once said she "fretted, pouted, and argued about her part" and "challenged my slaphappy way of shooting scenes."[125] Yet, his "slaphappy way of shooting" would win him the Oscar for Best Director. Not only that—his directing would win *her* Best Actress.

Americans absolutely loved the movie. It was a reversal of the Cinderella story. *Rich girl leaves rich man to marry poor reporter* sums it up pretty well. In a time when people were divided by their wealth or their lack of it, this plot gave people hope in humanity—in their innate worth.

It Happened One Night is known as one of the best romantic comedies of all time. The scene in which Claudette Colbert's character reaches out her leg to lure a car has become a staple in many other films. In one scene, the character Peter is seen stripping off his top, revealing a bare chest and no undershirt. For years, rumors spread that this scene alone led to the mass decline in undershirt sales across the United States, though the facts on that amusing anecdote remain decidedly murky.

So, you might think that the night in 1935 when Capra's film earned Best Picture, Best Director, Best Actor, Best Actress, and Best Adapted Screenplay is what made him such a Hollywood hero. However, he would walk along the nominees list for about another decade.

Two years after *It Happened One Night*, in fact, Capra heard his name called once again for Best Director at the Academy Awards—this time for his film *Mr. Deeds Goes to Town*.

We experience the movie through the eyes of Longfellow Deeds, a handsome man enjoying a simple existence in rural Vermont during the Great Depression, playing the tuba in his town's band. After the death of a distant uncle names him the beneficiary of a rather sizeable fortune, Deeds's rural rhythm is totally turned upside down as he's swept away to the big city, where he takes up many of the responsibilities central to his uncle's business and wealth. When the local newspaper catches wind of the young, seemingly naive billionaire, they decide to make headlines out of his off-kilter thinking and behavior.

Enter Louise "Babe" Bennett, who pretends to be a damsel in distress to stay close to Deeds and pen articles detailing his various states of faux pas. But in the classic Hollywood tradition, the longer she draws out her scheme, the more she falls in love with Deeds, and the deeper she stumbles into guilt and regret. Even though Bennett can't forgive herself and quits her job to save Deeds from further deceit, someone reveals Bennett's original intentions to Deeds nevertheless. He's absolutely crushed, and he picks up the pieces of his broken heart and prepares to return to the countryside.

But before he can leave, something extraordinary happens. While Deeds is moping around one night in doomed dejection, an old worker storms into the Deeds estate in a crazed frenzy of panic and despair, shouting that Deeds is disconnected from the foibles of the common man. He pulls a gun, only to collapse in a chair, appalled at the extremes to which his circumstances have pushed him. It's a tremendously melodramatic scene, but in Capra's careful and empathetic hands, it transforms into a delicately modulated moment in which for the first time, privileged and poor see each other as human beings rather than as conflicting social classes.

This thundering revelation is rendered quietly and sensitively—Deeds sees just how fortunate he really is and what a potent opportunity he has to change the world for the better rather than running at the first sign of the worst of it. Instead of continuing to mope at his love's betrayal, he decides to give away his fortune to the ailing people of the city. This move of borderline-ridiculous generosity sends Deeds's crooked financial handlers into a panic. In an attempt to maintain control of the fortune, they attempt to have Deeds declared insane, going so far as to set up a trial to try and prove to both judge and public just how cracked Deeds really is.

As he's assaulted by accusation after accusation, it's none other than Bennett's teary-eyed testimony that sells Deeds's sanity and integrity to the courtroom—she says that the only crime he ever committed was being kind. Can't get more Capra than that! The judge agrees with her case and lo and behold, Deeds gets the girl and is exonerated.

The character of Longfellow Deeds is the classic Capra

archetype—he's an eccentric living at his own scale, on his own time, and enjoying a blissful bubble of his own tastes. When we first meet him in the rural outlands of Mandrake Falls, he seems completely unfazed, perhaps even burdened, as if the notion of accepting $20 million— especially from an uncle he admits wasn't that close to him in the first place—is more weight than a simple man should care to bear. Here's a man who just wants a new mouthpiece for his tuba. Deeds's shameless quirkiness would be echoed in later Capra films like *You Can't Take It with You* (1938), but what distinguishes Longfellow Deeds is his gradually revealed soul. He's overwhelmed but not awestruck by the fortune, and he's not totally naïve—when his own advisors attempt to swindle him, he stands up for himself and his principles.

Mr. Deeds Goes to Town was a hit not only in the Academy voters' hearts—with six nominations and a Best Director win—but also in the box office, eventually grossing over $2 million.[126]

In 1938, Capra was nominated for Best Picture for his film *Lost Horizon*. Certainly an honor, but nothing like the acclaim he received for his previous projects. The film ended up creating serious debt for Harry Cohn of Columbia Pictures, making Capra, despite his prior success, not the most favored person in the studio.

Yet, like his other work, this film still holds significance and is even preserved in the National Film Registry. Many critics called the film a triumph. Frank S. Nugent of the *New York Times* said it was "a grand adventure film."[127] The *Hollywood Reporter* called it "an artistic tour de force."[128] Others noted how visually stimulating and captivating the film was.

Despite financial defeat, it took only a year for Capra to be walking about with the gold Oscar yet again, this time for his film *You*

Can't Take It with You (1938). Another potent tonic for the turmoil of the Great Depression, the film is essentially an indictment of the affluent sensibility in the form of a populist romantic comedy.

The story begins with a famous and powerful banker named Anthony P. Kirby, whose son, Tony Kirby (played by frequent Capra collaborator James Stewart), works beneath him. Anthony Kirby has plotted a route to further his industry aspirations, hampered by a minor hang-up: there's only one unsold house in a neighborhood in which Kirby plans to build a factory, and the owners of the house won't sell, no matter how much Kirby badgers them with his henchmen. This all is further complicated when it's revealed that Tony Kirby is dating a woman living in the house with her eccentric but adoring family.

After *You Can't Take It with You*, Capra was nominated for eleven Academy Awards, including Best Director in 1940 for his film *Mr. Smith Goes to Washington* (1939). He received acclaim and accolades for his documentaries, but it would be nearly seven years until Capra was on the nominee list again for one of his beautiful, irreverent narratives—a film that stands the test of time.

In 1947, Capra crossed the stage to accept his Academy Award for Best Director for the film *It's a Wonderful Life*, a Christmas movie that has been watched in American homes now for decades. Capra said of the work:

> I thought it was the greatest film I ever made. Better yet, I thought it was the greatest film *anybody* had ever made. It wasn't made for the oh-so-bored critics, or the oh-so-jaded literati. It was my kind of film for my kind of people.[129]

Elaborating further on its significance:

> *It's a Wonderful Life* sums up my philosophy of filmmaking. First, to exalt the *worth* of the individual. Second, to champion *man*—plead his causes, protest any degradation of his dignity, spirit or divinity. And third, to dramatize the viability of the individual—as in the theme of the film itself . . . There is a radiance and glory in the darkness, could we but see, and to see that we only have to look. I beseech you to look.[130]

Like *Mr. Deeds*, *It's a Wonderful Life* is centered around a man struggling with depression. However, unlike Deeds, the protagonist, family man George Bailey (James Stewart), has lost his entire fortune due to the Great Depression. As the story goes, it is Christmas Eve and Bailey is contemplating suicide. He is visited by a guardian angel named Clarence who shows him how terrible his family's lives would have been if he had never existed. Clarence shows George that regardless of the funds he provides for his family, he matters in far more profound ways than he realizes.

The movie came out right after World War II, when families were piecing their lives back together and reuniting with—or mourning—loved ones. Many soldiers were struggling with PTSD, which was not as publicly acknowledged as it is today.

The movie reinforces the idea that every life matters and every livelihood has value. This may be one of the most profound messages we can send out to people: *No matter what, we all make an impact in this world*.

The film also tackles issues such as mental health and the male gender role. Dialogue about these topics wasn't as prevalent as it is today, so mentioning them in a film was more than most were doing. Capra uses his lead to portray the stresses placed on fathers for being the sole providers—how they constantly have to make everything seem okay when it's not, and how they must appear all right even when they're not. A lot of men who returned from war, where bombs blasted around them and people were killed beside them, were expected to return to a normal, quiet routine. Though George Bailey isn't a war veteran (because he was refused entry due to a bad ear), he is a mental health veteran. And in a time where PTSD was common, this was a nod to the returning soldiers.

But what makes the film so subtly upending is the way it completely undermines more conservative perceptions of core American values. The centerpiece of those values is the idea of the self-made man—the family man who builds an empire just to support his wife and children. Media and advertising have built up the modern American male to be an ambitious individual who works hard, stays focused, builds his success, and provides for his family the things he may never have had when he was a child. This trope traces back to the origins of Americans as colonists—starting with nothing and creating an empire. Although in reality such success is not an attainable goal for everyone, especially in years after so much was given up and sacrificed for war, the question continued to weigh on the conscience—am I a failure because life is not what I dreamed it to be? What do I have to show for my limited time here on planet Earth? What mark did I leave?

That's not the definition of success Capra explores. He actively dismantles it by providing the audience with a character who wants to see the world and pave his own unique path through the doldrums of life. The viewer is forced to watch obstacle after obstacle chip away at those dreams as the years draw on.

The film is akin to the portrait of American success painted in Orson Welles's 1941 landmark work *Citizen Kane*. In that film, the life of a man is chronicled from his snow-dusted childhood innocence through his success as a newspaperman and his transformation into an inhuman monster turned ice-cold and callous from years of ego, indulgence, and detachment. In the end, Charles Foster Kane dies rich, famous, and depressingly hollow and sad. Meanwhile, George Bailey in *It's a Wonderful Life* has a head brimming with unfulfilled dreams and no job to speak of, but he's embraced by the warmth of his family and a community that respects him for his shimmering spirit and unflappable character. Charles Foster Kane ends as a tragic idea; George Bailey ends, in the eyes of Capra, as a true American hero: a loved man whose heart is left untarnished by the hardships of dutifully standing his post.

It was as if Capra's movies weren't movies at all, but rather wishes or challenges for the average citizen to dream bigger and behave better. In a world devastated by war and economic hardship, Capra's filmmaking gave audiences permission to see ordinary life for the extraordinary privileged that it is.

Capra's films were a gift to audiences, and they have returned the favor for nearly a hundred years in the form of undying admiration. The Academy agrees—to this day, Frank Capra is ranked with such revered company as William Wyler and John Ford as having more Best Director Academy Award wins than any other director—Ford had four wins, with Capra and Wyler tied for three.

It's somehow fitting that the film for which Capra is most

widely known, *It's a Wonderful Life*, didn't earn him any gold-plated statues on Oscar night. The film received a technical award for innovative practical effects, but even the screenwriter went home empty-handed. Which, if you ask me, does nothing but cement Capra as the people's filmmaker that he was. *It's a Wonderful Life* is yet another Capra work preserved in the National Film Registry for its cultural significance, and every Christmas season finds the film on such heavy rotation that it's nearly an American cultural punch line. Cinema history has granted the film, and its filmmakers, the honor that every artist aspires to—a certain degree of immortality.

Capra shows that artistry alone doesn't hit the mark; there needs to be strong entertainment, too. The audience needs to *need* the film. But if you can pull off both, as he at times achieved, message films can both sweep the awards shows and hit unparalleled box-office success.

Chapter 9

MEGA-IMPACT AND MEGA-BLOCKBUSTERS

Roger Ebert, the late Pulitzer Prize–winning film critic of Siskel & Ebert fame, once described the movies as "a machine that generates empathy."[131] And as we take a look in this chapter at the highest-grossing films of all time, a trend quickly emerges: the most successful films are very often the ones that most proudly bear their status as an empathy machine.

Empathy reveals itself as the language of the twenty-first century, and if that language has any recorded form, cinema proves be the most complete candidate. In its use of images, cinema communicates what text cannot—the impressions beneath mere words—and thus it connects people more easily and universally than any other medium. And with movies available through streaming, on-demand services, and theaters, they're arguably as accessible as any art form in history. One shot of a timeless screen presence like George C. Scott, Helen Mirren, or James Stewart can express the same multitudes as a hundred poeticisms from wordsmiths like Don DeLillo or T. S. Eliot.

The foremost goal of this chapter is to address the elephant in the room: Social Impact Entertainment versus commerce. Some films that set out to make a change are thought to be a form of nonprofit work. The impression is that art house, documentary, or sideline cinema doesn't concern itself at all with financial magnitude and instead seems to be operating on a different plane. But my aim is to flip this script. As we've seen with Frank Capra, Entertainment-Education or social impact filmmaking can be a valuable path to box-office success.

The power of story is sweeping entertainment that changes the world by laying bare essential issues that affect people across the globe. Changing the world is no longer a fringe endeavor; it's something for everyone, and nowhere is that more evident than the measurable impact both financially and culturally of the highest-grossing films over the past two decades.

Take a look at the worldwide gross of the top seven biggest box-office earners of all time.

1. *Avatar*, $2.85 billion
2. *Avengers: Endgame*, $2.80 billion
3. *Titanic*, $2.2 billion
4. *Star Wars: The Force Awakens*, $2.07 billion
5. *Avengers: Infinity War*, $2.05 billion
6. *Spider-Man: No Way Home*, $2 billion
7. *Jurassic World*, with its roaring dinosaurs pulling in a whopping $1.67 billion after fourteen years of silence from the franchise[132]

"Now hold the phone," you may be asking. "*Titanic*? *Avatar*, aka *FernGully* in space? *Star Wars*, of all things? How do these films count as Social Impact Entertainment?" For years, cynics have used the fact that audiences fork out millions for superfluous blockbusters like *Transformers* or the *Pirates of the Caribbean* sequels as evidence of mindless consumer culture and the death of intelligence in America. So when the same line of reasoning reveals that the general public repeatedly flocks to stories with something to say above all other types, how can that be ignored? When strictly looking at the numbers, the average moviegoer seems to be sending a very clear message: "We are smart and conscious creatures, and we respond to entertainment that exercises our capacity for human understanding in conversations that capture the global zeitgeist."

When smart moviegoers meet equally smart spectacle, ripples are made. When films with a message work best, they launch a dialogue with their audiences—a dialogue that continues long after people leave the cinema, creating word of mouth that ropes in new and old customers alike to confirm for themselves what all the fuss is about. That's not just a successful attempt at stirring the societal pot; it's a sound marketing tactic.

You may not have seen *Avatar* on its opening weekend. You may not have even seen it in its opening month (the film spent seven weeks at the number-one spot at the box office and fourteen weeks in the top ten[133]), but by its second week of release, there was barely a soul in the developed world who didn't know what it was, what it was about, and what people had to say about it. The same is true of *Star Wars: The Force Awakens*; by appealing to universal themes, it managed to tap into the collective fears and anxieties of those around the world while expanding the appeal of the *Star Wars* brand and making the mother of all franchises even more lucrative—all in one swoop.

Our top six Social Impact Entertainment films all made waves. With waves came critical acclaim, and with acclaim came awards and prestige. After months of trepidation and nervous press, they were all met with varying degrees of enthusiastic reviews. Combined, these films garnered a total of thirty Academy Award nominations, fourteen of which led to wins. Even Steven Spielberg, the father of the popcorn blockbuster, has achieved the best notices of his career whenever he's branched out into Social Impact Entertainment: He won Best Director Oscars for the Holocaust drama *Schindler's List* (1993) and the vivid WWII epic *Saving Private Ryan* (1998), and other historically and socially conscious films like *Lincoln* (2012) and *Bridge of Spies* (2015) consistently garnered accolades and esteem.

While this chapter focuses on blockbusters, we certainly want to recognize those who make films with a message for a narrow audience. Creating Social Impact Entertainment within a niche market is a noble effort. The power of story is a vast spectrum of approaches and intentions, all of which work to cut through the noise and facilitate empathy. In this chapter, we attempt to broaden the canvas and allow people to realize what some of the most successful filmmakers working today already know—overt social consciousness and mainstream entertainment are not mutually exclusive ideas, and for those who dare to combine the two, waves usually follow.

Avatar

Here we arrive at *Avatar* (2009), perhaps the ultimate Social Impact Entertainment blockbuster, the yardstick if ever there was one. It is one of those rare motion pictures that was not simply a record-breaking success—it put an exclamation point on the first decade of twenty-first-century filmmaking and became a semicolon for everything that would follow, both technically and theoretically. *Avatar* provoked thought, snickers, tears, and cynicism from all sides of the emotional spectrum in one massive stroke, and there hasn't been a film like it since. There may not be as many Na'vi costumes as there are Iron Man and Captain Kirk when it comes to media conventions, but in all other respects, *Avatar* has become a permanent fixture of movie royalty.

The film was the first in history to gross over $2 billion, staying at the number-one spot at the box office for seven weeks. As if that wasn't enough, to compensate for what director, writer, and producer James Cameron considered an interruption of momentum caused by Tim Burton's smash 3D hit *Alice in Wonderland*,[134] he prepared a new cut of the film with nine minutes of additional footage—comparatively, that re-release stumbled a bit, with a worldwide gross of $33 million.

The film's true main character, as James Cameron intended, is the extravagantly detailed environment of Pandora, and by allowing us to fall in love with it and become immersed, the movie had a very different kind of impact, one that was arguably more important than the immersion in a fictional planet: it put audiences back in touch with the natural world.

Any film that took more than ten years to arrive on the big screen ought to have such world-fixing ambitions. The film was James Cameron's first narrative since setting new high watermarks for financial success with *Titanic*. How exactly do you top the biggest film of all time, especially when it's your own movie you're attempting to best? By combining state-of-the-art visual effects, a prestige filmmaker with a worthy track record, and the secret weapon: an environmental agenda to serve as the project's lifeblood. Because whatever else you felt about *Avatar*—and chances are you've been vocal enough about it already one way or the other—you can't deny that its primary purpose revealed itself pretty early on: to serve as a bold, blunt-force statement about the abuse of natural landscapes and indigenous populations.

According to Cameron, the origins of Pandora reach all the way back to a treatment he wrote in the 1990s, but the director placed it on the back burner, thinking the world hadn't caught up to it technologically. It wasn't until 2006, when he felt computer technology had developed enough to bring his lush vision to life, that production finally began.

For James Cameron, the message was the purpose, not some by-product of the filmmaking process. Cameron felt that a certain kind of screen science fiction, a kind of cautionary cold shower of ideas once made by the likes of George Orwell and H. G. Wells, had dwindled since the success of *Star Wars*, a series that steered sci-fi toward more conventional mythological tropes. He felt that by making the film correctly he could, in a sense, have his cake and eat it too—the mythological story of heroes and villains, a hero's journey, serves as the "spoonful of sugar" to soften the audience toward the buried hysteria inspired by classic science fiction.

And as far as the critics were concerned, *Avatar* was a rousing success. The film was nominated for nine Academy Awards, and it garnered an 82 percent critical approval rating on the movie review aggregator Rotten Tomatoes.[135] Not only was it seen as painstakingly crafted entertainment but critics and audiences alike revered the shamelessness of its sociopolitical overtones. Roger Ebert raved about the film, suggesting that it was "predestined to launch a cult" and championed what he saw as its "flat-out Green and anti-war message."[136]

If only it had been embraced by everybody. *Avatar* caught as much backlash as it did praise. Notorious film critic Armond White penned an article in the *New York Press* dismissing James Cameron's intentions, questioning whether the groundbreaking spectacle and much-publicized 3D would distract audiences from the more sinister, hypocritical subtext: "Avatar is the corniest movie ever made about the white man's need to lose his identity and assuage racial, political, sexual and historical guilt."[137]

Too much? Arguably. But it was a sentiment that resonated with a vocal minority that threatened to stifle the majority's acclaim. One could wave the criticism away as the provocative reaching of an overzealous journalist (Armond White is a known troll in film criticism), but it speaks volumes about how much of their own beliefs people are willing bring into the screening room and how much skepticism some people have toward even the most earnest movies with a message.

The *Avatar* backlash also paints a picture of the state of impact cinema between the years 2000 and 2009. Progressive films like *Milk* (2008), *Brokeback Mountain* (2005), and yes, even *Avatar* were met with sneers and vitriol due to their attempt to tackle relevant issues. *Brokeback Mountain* was dismissed by many as "the gay cowboy "movie" and *Avatar* was the hippie-dippie environmentalist movie. Today, perhaps in part *because* of films like the aforementioned, both the public and the world of cinema have begun to embrace the power of story to transform.

Armond White's article was also indicative of a developing kind of journalistic takedown culture, often baited by films trying to say a little bit more. If somebody champions a movie as saying something important and of-the-now, it's good journalism (and good business) for somebody else to dissect that movie and, often through convolution and stubbornness, prove that it isn't as progressive as it claims to be, or that it's being progressive in a misguided or naive way. In his article, White was guilty of this: he deconstructed what was intended as an activist message and reduced it to the plight of the white man. Still others pointed out what they considered to be the irony of an anticapitalist film whose every facet feels machine-cut specifically for box-office success—and released by Fox, no less.

Compare the earnest and emotionally charged tree-hugging of *Avatar* to the brutal, blood-soaked landscapes of Alejandro González Iñárritu's *The Revenant* (2015). The films couldn't seem farther apart, but both are very different attempts to make the same kind of blockbuster. Both movies were touted by their creators as overt examples of message films, with Cameron emphasizing the rapturous beauty of nature, however foreign, and Iñárritu working overtime to convince you of the horror of man's treatment of the natural world. The films have comparable running times, and both deal in some measure or another with the exploitation of a world we essentially stole. But in *The Revenant*, these ideas are so deeply buried beneath director Iñárritu's vision (and borderline-fetishistic commitment to misery and violence) that the film becomes less like a reverie of life on Earth and a bit more like Mel Gibson's *The Passion of the Christ* (2004)—by the time the audience has come out the other side, they've been too numbed by the sheer spectacle of it all to remember what exactly they were supposed to take away.

The *Revenant*, too, suffered from skeptical reactions to its purported message, with many questioning why exactly the Native American characters were sidelined if the film's subtext was supposed to be about them. So despite its numerous Oscar wins (including Best Director, an award that eluded even *Avatar*) and star Leonardo DiCaprio's insistence during promotion that the film has a very distinct environmental stance, it is *Avatar* that has proven to be the most successful, both in the graceful voicing of its intentions and in its ability to touch and inspire people. When audiences emerged from *Avatar*, regardless of how they felt about the story, they were struck by the quiet beauty of the planet Pandora; when people left *The Revenant*, they perhaps remembered Leo getting mauled by a bear.

But that's merely one interpretation of *The Revenant*, just as it was Armond White's interpretation that *Avatar* was the CGI imagining of the white man's confession. Neither of these reactions tally up to a total failure to communicate. In fact, if the goal of impact cinema is to equip the public and make people more socially aware, the fact that these conversations happened at all means both movies were resounding successes. After all, bringing issues out in the open is really the point in the first place.

Cameron weighed in on the topic: "It has been very, very interesting for me in the last couple of months to see how many people have come to [my wife] Susie and myself asking if there is something we can do in association with *Avatar* because so many people around the world working with indigenous issues have seen their reality in the film—even though the film is a fantasy that takes place on a mythical world—people are seeing their reality through the lens of this movie."[138]

In an interview with Eric Ditzian for MTV News, James Cameron said of giving the script to Fox executives, "When they read it, they sort of said, 'Can we take some of this tree-hugging, "FernGully" crap out of this movie?' . . . And I said, 'No, because that's why I'm making the film.'"

In the same interview he went on to speak about the efficacy in *Avatar*, saying, "If you're tuned in to what's happening in 'Avatar,' you start to feel a sense of moral outrage when you see the tree fall [destroying the Na'vi's home], and it's a compassionate response for these people." He continued, "Then you feel a sense of uplift at the end as good vanquishes evil. If you put those two things together, it actually creates a ripe emotional matrix for people to want to do something about it."[139] And indeed it did. A myriad of environmental groups reported the number of volunteers spiking, and others created curriculum around the film. No better example of mega-blockbuster results and mega-impact.

Titanic

In 2012, fifteen years after it took theaters by storm, James Cameron's *Titanic* finally passed the $2 billion mark at the worldwide box office, becoming only the second film in history to reach the high water mark left by his own 2009 film *Avatar*. Cameron had retrofitted *Titanic* for a 3D rerelease to coincide with the hundredth anniversary of the eponymous disaster. The biggest movie of all time had returned, and it was greeted with warmth and nostalgia.

The fact that a movie only fifteen years old was even capable of capitalizing on reverence demonstrates just how rapidly *Titanic* penetrated the popular consciousness. It spawned both parodies and imitators, and it set a new benchmark for the American on-screen epic. During a behind-the-scenes feature for the extras on the 3D Blu-ray, James Cameron admitted to a fascination with the multigenerational impact of *Titanic*: "Parents were taking kids, and kids—adult kids—were taking their parents. It was this transgenerational sharing kind of experience, and people were really choosing who they wanted to experience the movie with, and I think the same thing could happen with this re-release."[140]

But before we discuss the rerelease, let's rewind a bit and study the premiere and everything that made it such a benchmark. Cast yourself back to the late 1990s. It was a decade of almost celebratory adolescence, one that Generation X would quickly call home. The populace harbored an anxiety, and they couldn't determine whether it would get worse or dissipate. The turn of the century was quickly approaching, and people weren't sure what to make of it. Writers like David Foster Wallace, Don DeLillo, and Chuck Palahniuk channeled this apprehension into some of the decade's defining literature (*Infinite Jest*, *Underworld*, and *Fight Club*, specifically), while filmmakers like Jonathan Demme, Clint Eastwood, Martin Scorsese, and Robert Zemeckis held up their end with *The Silence of the Lambs*, *Unforgiven*, *Goodfellas*, and *Forrest Gump*, among others.

Yet it was *Titanic*, a much-publicized Hollywood blockbuster, that came to define the decade at the box office. It achieved new heights by being the first film in history to gross over $1 billion worldwide.

During production, with every new piece of reportage, the movie seemed further destined for failure. The film's budget ballooned day by day, requiring two of the big-five studios,

Paramount and 20th Century Fox, to cover the costs. The cast was relatively unknown to mainstream Hollywood—Kate Winslet had only a few films, most notably Peter Jackson's independent gem *Heavenly Creatures*, under her belt, and Leonardo DiCaprio wasn't yet the box-office draw he was when he made films like *Gangs of New York* (2002) and *The Departed* (2006). The film seemed formfitted to the missteps of the notorious flops of the past. After all, there wasn't a soul alive who didn't already know how *Titanic* was going to end.

Further, the film wasn't even the first about the sinking of the Titanic. *A Night to Remember* by Roy Ward Baker, released in 1958, was revered as a classic by critics and film aficionados alike (although when it was released, curiously enough, it was considered a box-office flop). A half dozen other TV and film attempts on the subject didn't gain much traction either. So what was it that drew people to James Cameron's *Titanic* that wasn't deployed previously?

The key to its success lies not in its flowery detail but in the overarching flavor of fantasy that James Cameron spreads throughout the film, and in the almost machine-cut accessibility of virtually every character. Titanic is as lavish and historically accurate in its aesthetic as any epic of the last century, and the movie hits all the sociopolitical notes dealing with class that the original film did. The difference that sold people was the sense of sheen, soap, and Hollywood grandeur.

Titanic used an international tragedy as a template to tell a timeless love story that appeals to everybody—regardless of what deck you're on, you have a chance of being on that ship with Jack and Rose. If you grew up rich, you see yourself in Rose, who sits through tight-collared speeches and nods politely even when she feels she has so much to interject. If you grew up poor, you see yourself in Jack, who slips fearlessly aboard through a game of cards and the unbridled momentum of his own wanderlust. In the words of Cameron, "It doesn't matter that he doesn't have a dime. This is his ship, and his moment. He owns the moment."[141] As Rose said as a 100-year-old woman, "They called it the Ship of Dreams. And it was. It really was."

And that's the magic of the movie—it was less a recreation of a time and place and more a stylized evocation of the feeling of a time, the feeling of having nothing to lose and casting aside all trepidation in the name of a new, better life. For all its detail and commitment to the historical period, there's a reverence to *Titanic* that lends it the quality of a dream. Much like George Lucas with *Star Wars* before him, James Cameron was taking familiar ingredients and imbuing them with a fantasy he invited the audience to get lost in. It worked. Teenagers fell head over heels for the love story, while adults and elderly viewers got to indulge in a time that felt like a memory just out of reach.

This was proven at the box office. Not only did *Titanic* become the highest-grossing film of all time (until *Avatar*, nearly twenty years after its release), it remains the only movie in history to remain at the top of the box office for fifteen consecutive weeks (Spielberg's *E.T.* spent longer at number one, but its sixteen weeks were not consecutive). Even *Avatar* managed only half of that time at the top. The film did for James Cameron what *Star Wars* did for George Lucas in the 1970s—his name became synonymous with big, important cinema that you need to be paying attention to.

The genius of *Avatar*—and *Titanic* for that matter—is how skillfully Cameron created characters to connect with. Hitchcock described his films as beginning with the everyday person (though usually men) and then throwing them into a horrific or action-packed series of events that destabilizes their day-to-day life. The goal: to get the audience to see themselves on-screen, to connect, and as a result to increase efficacy, as noted by Sabido—the more people emotionally connect, the more compelled they are to action—whatever that may be.

What Cameron does differently than Hitchcock, though, is to provide not one but two models for an audience to engage with. In *Avatar*, the main character, Jake Sully (played by Sam Worthington), represents military "Hooyah" culture of dominate and control, while Neytiri (Zoe Saldana) represents an of-the-earth, hippie-esque, indigenous voice. Between these two extremes, you cover everyone on the spectrum—environmentalists to industrialists. *Titanic*, too, employs this brilliant structure, following two characters who embody both high culture and life on the lower decks. Through the love stories is where vision is shared and fused and where lessons are learned.

As Jack puts it in a passion-filled moment in *Titanic*, "They've got you in a glass jar like some butterfly, and you're goin' to die if you don't break out. Maybe not right away, 'cause you're strong. But sooner or later the fire in you is goin' to go out."

To which Rose responds, "It's not up to you to save me, Jack."

"You're right. Only you can do that."[142]

In both *Titanic* and *Avatar*, the structure of the film is about one character getting the other character to see the world through their eyes and reach a new truth as a result. For Rose, it's by walking and spitting off the upper decks of the *Titanic* or drinking and dancing with the Irish to her heart's content that she transcends the rules explicitly or inexplicitly conscripted onto her by class and gender roles. Can there be a stronger message than *live a life of your own making*? In cultures where class is explicit—as in India, where marriage is often pressured and arranged—or beneath the surface—as it is in the US—it's a theme that resonates globally to create a world where we all can be, as William Ernest Henley put it in his poem "Invictus," the master of our fate, the captain of our soul.[143] It's no wonder that *Titanic* blew the lid off what was possible at the box office.

Star Wars

Nobody can deny the permanent stamp *Star Wars* has left on the world. Upon its inception as a pulp science-fiction series, it exploded into a cornerstone of pop culture and unquenchable fandom. And in its own unified way, it's also the largest impact franchise in movies, using a classic mythos of good and evil and choosing one's own destiny to deliver weary audiences a blast of pure-hearted optimist spectacle.

The deeper message woven into said spectacle, however, was something that George Lucas was concerned about in the years preceding *Star Wars'* release. And it was this message that made audiences fall in love with the film, see it repeatedly, consume its brand in record fashion, and share it all again with their kids.

The first three films in the nine-part franchise earned about $2 billion collectively. Six months after its release, the first film, *A New Hope*, premiering in 1977, surpassed Steven Spielberg's *Jaws* (1975) as the highest-grossing film of all time. *The Force Awakens* (2015), the seventh film in the series, this time by Disney, still sits as the fourth-highest-grossing film of all time at over $2 billion.[144] If ticket-buying audiences speak with hard-earned money, the signal is crystal clear: *Star Wars* knew how to strike a very specific chord like few other film franchises in history. Forty years after the original film's release, people attend conventions in swarms in full Chewbacca garb, and to some, *Star Wars* is like a religion.

In the 1977 TV special *The Making of Star Wars*, Lucas, then 33, credits the film's positivity as its primary source of success, saying to the camera that "it has heroes and villains, and . . . essentially is a fun movie to watch. It's been a long time since people have been able to go to the movies and see a sort of straightforward, wholesome, fun adventure."[145]

Indeed it had been a long time. The tempo of the 1960s was films benumbed, frightened, divided, and in search of moral absolution. The '60s saw both the Cold War and the Vietnam War amidst the hippie movement and its sometimes chilling offshoots like Charles Manson's Helter Skelter.

In the early '70s, the hippie dream seemed to come to an end. The dark heart of the world seemed strangely comfortable in broad daylight, and the films being made during this time reflected that—*A Clockwork Orange* (1971), *Dirty Harry* (1971), *The French Connection* (1971), *The Godfather* (1972), *Mean Streets* (1973), and *Taxi Driver* (1976), to name a few.

To provide an antidote to all this grimness, Lucas sought inspiration from the shoot-'em-up Westerns and serialized adventures of his childhood. He wanted to give a new generation the same kind of rip-roaring adventure classics that formed him as a young boy, like the Tarzan and John Carter of Mars stories. So after several drafts of the script, he gradually created what had less to do with heady intellectualism like his prior film *THX 1138*—which invoked aspects of George Orwell's *1984* and Aldous Huxley's *Brave New World* and which audiences didn't respond to—and more like the pulpy, space-opera thrills of *Flash Gordon*. In a way, he was shifting the scales from perhaps an 80 percent message-heavy narrative to Sabido's 20 percent in a manner to engage and hold audiences. At the center of all that spectacle was the unifying mysticism of destiny, the hero's quest, and of course, the all-encompassing power of The Force.

The Force, as the film defines it, is essentially a nebulous, spiritual component to the fabric of the universe. To quote Obi-Wan Kenobi, "it's an energy field created by all living things; it surrounds us, penetrates us; it binds the galaxy together."[146] The Force is, by design, a naturally appealing idea to virtually all cultures and religions, in their desire to see some transcendent, connecting thread throughout the human experience. In an interview for the 1988 documentary series *Joseph Campbell and the Power of Myth*, Lucas tells the series' producer, journalist Bill Moyers, that he saw *Star Wars* as "taking all of the issues that religion represents and trying to distill them down into a more modern and more easily accessible construct that people can grab onto to accept the fact that there is a greater mystery out there."[147]

If you look at the mechanics of the proliferation of religion and the success of *Star Wars*, you'll notice some pretty surprising parallel threads. In order to understand them a bit more clearly, let's first discuss why it is that religion has remained such an enduring part of the human social paradigm.

Richard Dawkins coined the term *meme* in his 1976 book on evolutionary biology, *The Selfish Gene*, to explain the success of lasting social forces such as religion. As Dawkins defined it, a meme is a unit of culture, and that unit affects the well-being of groups in the same way genes facilitate certain traits in individual organisms. So if a new cultural trend, analogous to biological mutation, assists in the endurance of a society through a kind of sociological natural selection, that trend is more likely to be adhered to by a population, therefore increasing the survivability of each individual creature and, in turn, the species as a whole.

This understanding provides us with insight into what makes religion so successful. Regardless of the flavor, it's a catalyst around which people can come together, communicate, and work to advance. Virtually all enduring religions throughout history—from Christianity to Islam to Judaism—have contained unifying elements of adventure, morality, the stark contrast of good and evil, a messiah, the afterlife, and a guiding force that provides sense and locomotion to all existing things. There doesn't, however, appear to be a God at the center of *Star Wars*. That's part of the genius of the series: George Lucas constructed a mythos that was vague enough not to be blasphemous but universal enough in its mysticism to appeal to anybody looking to surrender to a power greater than himself.

Star Wars doesn't espouse the existence of an almighty deity or even dictate what morality is beyond expressing that it lives in a delicate balance. In fact, at the start of the first film, The Force is a outdated concept steeped deeply in skepticism, and that's what pushes people toward it—by design, the film challenges you to shed your crusty exterior and relinquish yourself to something mysterious in order to gain an understanding of how the universe functions. What else is religion in its muscle fibers if not that?

Whether or not you believe in God, Jesus, Allah, or Zeus is all part of your individual journey, but every journey is connected by a desire to find what lies beyond our immediate perception of things, and what it all means, if anything in the slightest. *Star Wars*, like religion, sought to unite by espousing hope and giving people something to believe in.

That unity didn't simply succeed; it spanned decades, generations, even continents. One would be hard pressed to find a part of the developed world that hasn't been touched by *Star Wars* in some measurable way. The series has been passed down from one generation to another, and now yet again through its new life with Disney. For many people, watching *Star Wars* with their children for the first time is an essential act of contemporary family bonding. In 2007, the Los Angeles City Council named May 25 "*Star Wars* Day" to commemorate the thirtieth anniversary of the first film's release. Four years later, a group of fans in Canada launched the first organized *Star Wars* Day celebration (on May 4, a pun on the saying "May the force be with you"), and since then fans across the globe have celebrated the holiday annually.

From 1999 to 2005, three more films were launched, adding to the existing trilogy. The first of these, *The Phantom Menace*, broke the single-day gross record of *Jurassic Park* by racking up over $28 million on its first day of release, and it eventually went on to make more than $1 billion worldwide.[148] Why such earth-shattering success? Regardless of what you think of the quality of *The Phantom Menace* (1999), *Attack of the Clones* (2002), and *Revenge of the Sith* (2005), at the end of the day they were still *Star Wars* films, and to most people, that was all that needed to be said. With the original entries in the franchise, released between 1977 and 1983, the words

Star Wars became synonymous with the kind of innocent, wondrous adventure people have expected from movies ever since.

So after two generations of world-sweeping influence, the success of the series' seventh installment, *The Force Awakens*, was perhaps a shock to nobody, but it was nonetheless a relief to audiences and distributors. The film had quite a bit riding on it, not least what many viewed as the integrity of the franchise—it was the first live-action *Star Wars* film in a decade and the first since Disney purchased Lucasfilm in 2012. Lifelong fans were anxious about whether the soul established in that first film would be preserved in such corporate hands.

So the biggest question when it came time to produce Episode VII was, who should Disney pick to carry on that tradition? Well, who else but Hollywood golden child and bona fide fanboy J. J. Abrams? After two financially successful (and critically acclaimed) motion-picture reboots of the *Star Trek* universe, the announcement of Abrams's involvement with *The Force Awakens* felt like a natural next step for the filmmaker, with critics such as Mark Kermode[149] and the crew of Spill.com[150] going so far as to call the action-oriented *Star Trek into Darkness* an audition to direct the next *Star Wars* film.

The title of the film, *The Force Awakens*, doubles as a description of both the plot and the intentions of the film itself; after three entries in the saga during the 2000s, episode VII attempted to reengage the series with its hopeful, adventurous roots. Beneath the commitment to practical non-CGI effects and on-location 35mm photography was a desire to reinstate the franchise to the pure-hearted characters, spiritual reach, and a genuine sense of wonder and possibility that struck people so profoundly in that first film. In an interview with *Wired*, J. J. Abrams described his intentions by saying that the original *Star Wars* "both allowed the audience to understand a new story but also to infer all sorts of exciting things that might be. In that first movie, Luke wasn't necessarily the son of Vader, he wasn't necessarily the brother of Leia, but it was all possible . . . That was really the only requirement [screenwriter Lawrence Kasdan] and I imposed on each other: The movie needed to be delightful. It was not about explaining everything away, not about introducing a certain number of toys for a corporation, not about trying to appease anyone. This has only ever been about what gets *us* excited."[151]

It also provided the series yet another chance to jack into the changing public consciousness. If the original *Star Wars* united people through hope and spiritual themes, Episode VII united people through nostalgia, conversation, and—like the original, in the form of a strong heroine, Princess Leia—representation.

J. J. Abrams, while acknowledging that women have always enjoyed *Star Wars*, stated that he felt the movies still were marketed more toward boys than girls, and he wanted *Star Wars* to be a property for everyone. In an interview with Ricky Camilleri at AOL Studios, Abrams said that *Star Wars* "should be for everyone. That's the whole point . . . As the father of a daughter as well as two sons, I wanted this movie to be something where Leia wasn't the only girl . . . I really wanted to make sure that this movie felt a little bit more equal in that regard."[152] So he cast English newcomers Daisy Ridley (playing Rey), an actress with no previous feature film experience, and John Boyega (playing Finn), whose role in the acclaimed 2011 sci-fi comedy *Attack the Block* was one of his only previous film credits, to lead the mother of all franchises.

The inclusion of Rey as the lead character was a revelation not just for *Star Wars* but for big-budget blockbusters in general. Rather than being driven by a princess or a love interest, the film featured a forthright, rounded character whose primary ambition, like the trendsetting Luke Skywalker before her, was to traverse the cosmos and realize her destiny. The film flips the conventional damsel-in-distress trope completely on its head: throughout the film, it is in fact Rey who regularly saves her male counterparts, usually adding an amusing quip on the rescue's coattails.

In the film's ultimate set piece, a beautifully choreographed duel of lightsabers in the snow, who is called upon to challenge the film's villain, Kylo Ren, during the climax? Not Finn, as the series' succession of male heroes would suggest, but Rey. Unprecedented for a central female character, Rey gets the privilege of wielding what is perhaps cinema's most iconic weapon, and though she struggles, she ultimately holds her own against Kylo Ren.

In a panel discussion published in the *Guardian*, contributor Sara Galo reflected on the history of female characters in *Star Wars*: "Leia and Rey are the heroines I needed so desperately as a child, but I'd argue that Rey is even more important: without the trappings of a royal title, she is paving the way towards placing more women in superhero roles."[153]

At a White House conference on gender diversity in toys and media, Tasia Filippatos, at the time the senior vice president for communications at Disney Consumer Products, confirmed that the inclusion of a woman in a central role was very intentional: "That was purposeful on Disney's part and purposeful from the filmmaker's perspective to make that lead character a strong empowered female."[154] And it wasn't just a creative choice—it was something that was designed to reap as much financial benefit as possible: "*Star Wars* has always been one of those franchises that absolutely crossed gender—it covered all demographics," Filippatos said. "But the product line, historically, has been very very boy focused and was very much geared towards boys despite the fact that these were characters that resonated very strongly with all parts of the population."[155]

And it worked. From gender to race, these overt Social Impact Entertainment elements were the perfect catalyst for generating even more publicity and word-of-mouth buzz on the shoulders of what Disney marketing was churning out. Typing "The Force Awakens feminism" into Google unleashes a landslide of articles, blog posts, and videos discussing the empowering, feminist elements of the film. One blogger wrote a piece accusing the movie of being a long piece of social justice propaganda.[156] Was there any truth to that? The only way to know for sure was to buy a ticket and see for yourself.

Fortunately for Abrams and Disney, people did precisely that in outrageous numbers. *The Force Awakens* didn't just return the franchise to its record-breaking glory; it became the third movie in history at the time to pass the $2 billion mark at the box office. It also earned the franchise some of its best reviews since *Return of the Jedi*, with a "Certified Fresh" score of 92 percent from the movie-review aggregator Rotten Tomatoes and a Metacritic score of 80. By casting a woman and a Black man in the lead roles, *The Force Awakens* didn't just reinvigorate the brand—it transcended social barriers, opened the series to several new audiences, and primed the saga for the franchise's new life. In fact, with so many news pieces dissecting the movie's social commentary and impact, going to the movie became a small act of social justice in and of itself—a chance to participate in a global conversation about an important issue—representation, and how we can innovate our stories young and old to better reflect and include our diverse world.

The Avengers: Endgame and Infinity Wars

Let's throw out a few names: Iron Man. Captain America. Thor. Black Panther. If you plucked a collection of random strangers off the street twenty years ago and asked who any of these characters were or what their background was, surely no more than 25 percent of them would be able to tell them apart, let alone explain their personalities and motivations. Captain America. That's the guy with the shield, right? I love the shield guy! Oh, wait, Thor. Hold on, I've got this. Isn't he the guy with the giant hammer?

In the last seventy-five years, comic book superheroes have gone from the funny pages to the silver screen, turning caped crusaders and related characters into some of the most widely circulated and revered intellectual property known today.

Even if you're not a cinephile, walking into a multiplex, you'll be quick to notice that there's hardly a week that goes by without at least one screen being occupied by a Marvel movie or a superhero film in general. It's an extension of a new worldwide paradigm. In the same way the ancients shaped their culture around their deities (who they didn't necessarily believe were anything other than fiction), human beings in the twenty-first century have started shaping their culture around characters from comics and superhero flicks. How different is an ancient statue of Zeus in a public place from a sprawling billboard of Doctor Strange looming large over the citizens of a massive city like New York or Los Angeles? And further—what do these superheroes say about us, and how do they give meaning and purpose to our individual lives as well as the collective zeitgeist?

Before we get ahead of ourselves, let's ask a fundamental question: what are superheroes? To the uninitiated, a superhero might just be an overly idealistic person in a cape who saves kittens stuck in trees and occasionally protects the Earth from interstellar invasions. But a more comics-savvy individual might have a very complex, personal answer cultivated from years of obsessive reading and encyclopedic understanding. This is an indication of the passion society has developed for its superheroes. These characters are people—some human, some not—with extraordinary abilities who become, through their trials and tribulations, the faces of certain values, flaws, strengths, and virtues. After all, what three values did Superman fight for in the face of abject peril time and time again? Truth, justice, and the American way.

Few things embody the prevalence of superheroes better than the Marvel Cinematic Universe (MCU). A vast collection of more than twenty films released since 2008, these movies sought to push the boundaries of screen storytelling past the trends that more cynical viewers mocked.

People complained of too many uninspired sequels? How about a series of movies, some similar, some totally different, following characters that are related but often vastly separated, as part of a larger story? It seems like a bold proposition, but it's not without precedent. It's not too different from the literature of J. R. R. Tolkien. He wrote many works beyond *The Hobbit*, but while each was a self-contained story, they all provided a unique window into the greater universe of Middle-earth. Another example in both literature and film: J. K. Rowling's *Harry Potter*. A series of seven books and eight films work together like gears in a stopwatch to not only tell a story but also create an entirely new world with its own rules, customs, and values. The same is true of the MCU—rather than making a series of films that continue for purely monetary reasons, producer and Marvel CEO Kevin Feige sought to create blockbusters that were portals into a much more vast and intricately detailed universe.

Comic books have been a part of American culture since their inception in 1934, when what we know as the first comic book was published as *Famous Funnies*, a compilation of previously printed strips, segments, and stories of various titles. Those were halcyon days of much simpler interests—"comics" were short one-to-three-panel strips, often funny or satirical, thus the name *comic* book.

The comics of Marvel function like Sabido's soap operas—through a serialized format, readers can gradually attach themselves to characters who are just like them. But comics encountered some difficulty in being taken seriously as a potent storytelling medium. They originated as novelties, short-form curiosities that compelled readers to flip through just a few more pages of the daily newspaper. But this was not without precedent. On the side of film, even the Lumière brothers weren't convinced of the medium's legitimacy, with the groundbreaking duo declaring early on that it didn't have much life beyond county fairs and public displays. It wasn't until people like D. W. Griffith and Sergei Eisenstein saw potential in it as both a formal and a dramaturgical treasure trove that cinema was gifted with the aura of respectability and even reverence it now possesses.

Comic books haven't traveled exactly the same path. Even now, comics are seen by many as something to entertain the fledgling minds of children rather than the mature sensibilities of grown-ups. It took an entire generation of kids bringing the genre out into the world as adults for it to really hit the limelight, skyrocketing to international fame those most notably responsible for its success: Jack Kirby, Steve Ditko, and Stan Lee.

Those familiar with his legacy and character remember Stan Lee as the white-haired, bespectacled gentleman with cameos in almost every superhero movie since the early 2000s, but in 1939 Lee was just a sixteen-year-old kid from the Bronx looking for a job. As if fate itself had planned it, it was this same year that Timely Comics, one of the first major entities of the early-to-mid-twentieth-century comics boom, had only just found its footing as an organization. Back then, the name *Marvel Comics* belonged to a line of supernatural stories and characters published by Timely—far from the independent company we know it to be today. Through family connections, Lee was hired by Timely as an assistant, learning the trade of comic writing from daily first-hand observation, and over the course of decades, he slowly ascended the ranks from filling coffee orders to writing his very own stories. Lee was later joined by illustrators Steve Ditko and Jack Kirby. Starting in the early '60s, the three artists shed the skin of Timely Comics and transformed it into something resembling its contemporary Marvel image. Their first title? None other than *The Fantastic Four*. The story of a space exploration gone mutant would be followed by other, similar titles, notably *Uncanny X-Men* and, perhaps the most iconic comic Stan Lee was ever associated with, *The Amazing Spider-Man*.

The man inside the spider suit, Peter Parker, is a synecdoche for all that Lee, Ditko, and Kirby aspired to achieve with their comic book renaissance. Spider-Man is the gold standard in relatable comic book characters. He isn't a god, like Thor, tearing down armies with a swing of his mighty hammer, nor is he Batman, an emotionally lacerated millionaire harboring secrets too dark for any sane creature. Peter, in almost every iteration of the character, is just a high school student. He's not a scientific genius—he does well in school and spends his pre-Spider-Man time pursuing a career in physics—but unlike the Fantastic Four's Reed Richards, he's not the smartest man in the world. He's just smart in ways the majority of people can realistically aspire to, or at least relate to. He's good looking, but only at a glance, and not enough to prevent him from tasting bully Flash Thompson's fist on a regular basis. He's just handsome enough to suggest that behind every geeky, socially awkward exterior lies someone with qualities buried by our superficial judgments.

Perhaps most crucially, Peter Parker is just a teenager. He isn't Superman, flying high above the clouds, detached from human foibles. Peter Parker doesn't even have life figured out. In the shuffle of his daily routine, balancing school, his relationship with his aging Aunt May, and the crime-fighting responsibilities of your friendly neighborhood Spider-Man, his mutant powers are simply one more shadow of the adulthood he's still learning how to face. In fact, at a certain point in the comics, and indeed the film *Spider-Man 2* (2004), Peter Parker gives up his red-and-blue mantle, deciding he can't bear the weight of the world on his tiny shoulders any longer. That kind of doubt and emotional exhaustion make him accessible to virtually all age groups. In a sense, we're all teenagers learning to adapt to our own powers and weaknesses and the responsibilities of wielding them. No matter how grown up or mature a person is, nobody has all the answers. Nobody is perfect. Not even Spider-Man. So maybe it's okay to forgive yourself for occasionally failing to strike the right balance all the time.

Another great example of relatable characters are the X-Men, an early comic creation of Lee, Ditko, and Kirby. The story of a school of mutants might seem like nothing more than inspiration for adolescent pop entertainment, and in a way, it is. But look more closely at these characters, and you'll see metaphors for a cornucopia of social issues that continue to define the human experience. In the world of *X-Men*, people hate mutants, pick on them, and ostracize them for qualities that were in no way their choosing—just part of their natural DNA. They are discriminated minorities in the same way people of color, homosexuals, and trans people have been throughout history.

By flipping the script on what it means to be different, the X-Men embraced representation and diversity, making oddity itself a sign of power and what it means to be super. These essential elements allowed readers and movie-goers to connect to their superheroes through their own struggles and later provided box-office success as well. But the failures were numerous.

Ever since Tim Burton first brought Batman to mainstream film life in 1989, people have been clamoring to get the superhero formula right. That meant sitting though *Spawn* (1997), a CGI-plastered mess with admirable-but-unrealized ambitions; Roger Corman's *The Fantastic Four*, made on the cheap in 1994 solely to maintain the film rights to the characters, and so stunningly poor that it was never theatrically released; and even the oversexed 1996 Pamela Anderson vehicle *Barb Wire*, in which Anderson plays a crime-fighting nightclub dancer with risible results.

It was a knockout one-two punch in the early 2000s that finally showed people what the equation really was: a combination of Bryan Singer's *X-Men* in 2000 and Sam Raimi's *Spider-Man* in 2002. Both films featured an associate producer who would become instrumental not only in the success of future superhero films but also in propelling the blockbuster itself into the next stage of its evolution: Kevin Feige.[157]

Kevin Feige has been a film nut practically since birth. When he was a teenager, he figured out that his heroes, Hollywood giants like Ron Howard, Robert Zemeckis, and none other than George Lucas, had all gone to the same film school, the USC School of Cinematic Arts. Film school was perhaps inevitable, but for Feige, being accepted into USC's program meant joining the pantheon, and for the fledgling producer, nothing less was acceptable. He applied for the program five times and was rejected each time. Family, friends, and mentors tried to soften the blow, suggesting that perhaps he could attend the school studying another subject; to Feige, they were out of their minds. And as is almost always the case with media legends, persistence was the key to success—on his sixth application, Feige was finally accepted into the program, paving the way for the decades of success to come.

His producing résumé started somewhat thin, serving as assistant to other producers on titles like *Volcano* and *You've Got Mail*, far cries from the blockbusters he'd guide in the future. But the same resilience that got him into USC would open the doors to Marvel Studios. In 2000, the company brought Feige on board as they attempted to carve an identity in the filmmaking landscape of the new millennium. Feige, beneath the varnish of confident professionalism, was a devoted comics nerd—who better to help decide how to creatively steer a comic book adaptation than someone who's a devotee himself?

After his early success with *Spider-Man* and *X-Men*, Feige proposed something that had never been truly realized in blockbuster film, and especially not in the superhero genre. To mirror the various storylines of the comic books they were based on, Feige proposed creating a cinematic universe, one in which all superheroes occupied the same reality, even if they weren't all on-screen at the same time. Each one would stand alone as a film—with its own ideas, themes, and characters—and also serve as a tile in a much grander storytelling mosaic. People so desperately cling to the idea that cinema is bloated with too many sequels, remakes, reimaginings—here was a way of making films that were both original (well, as original as an adaptation can be) and part of an ongoing franchise.

The film that kicked off the entire endeavor was 2008's *Iron Man*. Although history has cemented it as a bona fide hit, grossing more than half a billion dollars worldwide, the film's success rendered it somewhat of a dark horse. At the time of its release, the character of Iron Man wasn't nearly as widely known as Batman, Spider-Man, or Superman. It also starred Robert Downey Jr., who had spent years away from the spotlight embroiled in drugs, alcohol, and various bouts of jail time and rehabilitation. Its director was Jon Favreau, who, despite having proven his competency both as a writer and as a filmmaker, had yet to prove himself as a helmsman of titanic successes. His first true hit was the 2003 Will Ferrell Christmas comedy *Elf* (hardly a precursor to the thrills of *Iron Man*), and his previous film, *Zathura: A Space Adventure* (2005), a surreal fantasy about a magic board game, failed to recoup its budget at the box office. But even though a failure would have meant the immediate ruins for Marvel, the creative crew persevered. It turned out to be just the right combination of wild card elements to add up to one of those so-crazy-it-just-might-work ideas. Plus, the story was too compelling to be collecting dust on a shelf next to countless other unrealized projects.

Tony Stark, a physics-genius-turned-billionaire-playboy who develops remorse after a lifetime of developing weapons, isn't exactly relatable in his abilities or in his resources, but he distinguishes himself from most other superheroes by being a person, first and foremost. He isn't quite the pristinely positive model of behavior he might be in the hands of someone like Miguel Sabido, but that's part of what makes him so interesting. He's selfish, he's infantile, he's even a bit self-destructive, but he's also razor-sharp and has a verbal quiver loaded with those perfect comebacks regular minds so rarely have when needed most—not to mention possessing a genuine heart beneath the veneer of luxury and snark. Like Peter Parker, Tony Stark struggles with all the personal setbacks that hamper even the most secure human being.

And those setbacks turned into the film's greatest asset. *Iron Man* wasn't just a success—it proved to be one of the freshest entries in the superhero genre since Sam Raimi's *Spider-Man*. Robert Downey Jr.'s portrayal of Tony Stark, the billionaire-genius who turned from war profiteer into defender of the public, proved to be a perfectly synthesized alloy of the conflicted pathos of the character and Downey Jr.'s own freewheeling personality. The result was one of the most compelling screen characters not just of the Marvel Cinematic Universe, not just of the superhero genre, but arguably of all time. He and Jon Favreau's spin on the story so perfectly balanced the massive pyrotechnics and the spiky, self-aggrandizing humor that Downey Jr. naturally exuded, creating a slick, thrilling adventure that made you laugh as often as you gritted your teeth.

Iron Man was followed by several further films establishing the first "phase" of the Marvel Cinematic Universe; *The Incredible Hulk* (2008), a reboot that scrapped an earlier, less well-regarded film about the Hulk directed by Ang Lee; *Captain America* (2011), telling its story of Steve Rogers, a scrawny aspiring soldier with arms like twigs but a heart of gold; and of course, *Thor* (2011), the tale of a Norse god banished from his home realm of Asgard to learn humility among Earth-bound mortals. All of these films featured star-studded casts and creative crews, many of whom had never ventured into superhero territory before—even director Kenneth Branagh, known primarily for his dense and faithful Shakespearean adaptation, came in to lend his lavish touch to *Thor*.

Titanic be damned—if there's anything that will weld posteriors into theater seats, it's a high-wire brawl featuring an intergalactic band of misfits. In 2012, four years after the release of *Iron Man*, the world was gifted something many comic geeks had relegated to the status of pipe dream: *The Avengers*, a two-and-a-half hour rip-roaring spectacle featuring not one, not two, but a whopping *six* superheroes banding together to fight. Feige brought in director Joss Whedon, known for lending a sensitive-yet-quirky touch to TV series like *Buffy the Vampire Slayer* and *Dollhouse*. Someone primarily known for small-screen glory might not seem like the natural pick for something as unprecedented as *The Avengers*, but it proved to be the perfect choice: television requires a certain amount of sprawl, juggling, and acrobatic narrative surgery to bring a multi-episode series to a coherent close, and the same is certainly true of a movie with six superheroes. Each character needed to have a distinct depth and development without crowding against other characters or drawing too much screen time away from the sweeping scope of alien attacks and a universe in turmoil.

The results shattered the very Earth the fictional heroes were intended to protect, grossing more than $600 million domestically and $1.5 billion worldwide. The film created a brand-new superhero paradigm. In fact, the formula was so successful that several attempts have been made by other companies and properties to accomplish the same goal, often to less successful ends. DC Comics, the Microsoft to Marvel's Apple, teamed with Warner Bros. to establish its own cinematic universe, starting with *Man of Steel* (2013) and culminating in *Justice League (2017)*, DC's less successful answer to the super hero mashup of *The Avengers*. In a desperate stab to follow the trend, even Universal attempted to create its own cinematic "Dark Universe" by planning a series of reboots based on classic horror properties, including *The Mummy* and *Frankenstein*. The former, released in 2017, bombed so spectacularly that plans for *Bride of Frankenstein*, which would have starred *No Country for Old Men*'s Javier Bardem as the creature of legend, were shelved indefinitely.[158] Trends produce many imitators, but in the realm of hyperlink franchise filmmaking, Marvel achieved something that has yet to be reproduced.

The Avengers was followed by three installments: *Avengers: Age of Ultron* (2015), again helmed by Joss Whedon; *Avengers: Infinity*

War (2018); and *Avengers: Endgame* (2019), each one adding more characters than the last. By the time the series reached *Endgame*, the cast had inflated to an unparalleled roughly three dozen on-screen superheroes, all established by twenty-one feature films released over the course of ten years, including *Doctor Strange*, *Ant-Man*, and *Black Panther*. Watching *Infinity War* and *Endgame* really impresses upon you the sense of a Tower of superhero Babel, where all things from all places merge into a single narrative melting pot.

In the months leading up to such a dizzying clash of titans with each new *Avengers* installment, many were concerned that the undertaking might be too massive to produce a coherent piece of storytelling. Yet the franchise continued to garner both box-office success and positive reviews from critics. *Infinity War* grossed a world-igniting sum of more than $2 billion worldwide, making it not only the highest-grossing film of its year but also the fourth highest-grossing movie ever, only to be passed by *Endgame* a year later. *Endgame* would go on to do a whopping $2.8 billion worldwide to become the highest-grossing film of all time, beating out *Avatar* before it had even left theaters.[159]

The MCU is now one of those cultural forces that's too massive to slip quietly into the night. Tallying up the grosses of all Marvel's films from *Iron Man* to *Endgame* to *Spider-Man: No Way Home*, the franchise has grossed over $27 billion across the globe, and with DVD and streaming, that number will only continue to grow. This spectacular series, and all the films it encompasses, is here to stay. It has slipped its way into both cinematic history and the very fabric of popular culture. In the wake of such a massive footprint, it's very easy to imagine a world where these characters are considered as essential to understanding human history as the works of Shakespeare and F. Scott Fitzgerald's *The Great Gatsby*. How far will our relationship with such enormous movies go?

On that note, let's halt for a moment and retread something important. In earlier chapters, we discussed in looser terms the ways in which stories are the backbones of cultural understanding. Human beings have been on Earth for around two hundred thousand years, and in that time, we've used stories of gods, demons, and messiahs not only to explain the world around us but to provide the basis for entire systems of morality. A perfect example of this is the Bible. It's both a moral yardstick and a step-by-step explanation of how the universe as we know it came to be.

In its earliest chapters, those assembled prior to the birth and life of Jesus, the Bible tells the story of how God created the world in seven days—first the Earth; then the stars that surround it so beautifully in the nighttime; then the first man, Adam, from the very dust produced by the Earth; then the first woman, Eve, from Adam's rib. Through the Tree of Knowledge, the couple's immaturity and selfishness created shame and deceit and damned the entire human race to be born in sin. The rest of the book is a guide to ridding ourselves of that sin in the form of fables and historical events. When we finally read about the birth of Jesus, he becomes the moral compass for all humankind, and his death by crucifixion frees all of humankind from the curse of Adam and Eve's original sin. Although civilization has begun to take the creation stories less literally—science has advanced enough to formulate factually accurate theories of how the universe formed and how life on Earth came to be—the ideals the stories encapsulate are still tightly adhered to by people all over the world, two thousand years after the birth of Jesus.

What if it was suggested that *The Avengers* was the newest cultural mythology to shape and propel us further? It might seem ridiculous to some, seeing as comic books are barely considered art in more elitist circles, let alone mythology to rival the likes of Greece and Egypt. After all, the majority of what we consider mythologies have hundreds if not thousands of years on *The Avengers*—throughout history, many monarchical societies, including England, have held institutions of worship in equal if not greater esteem than royalty. How can people in leotards and masks even dream of coming close to that? What does any of it mean in the context of mythology and religion, for that matter?

Think about the role that mythology and religion play in society. From their ideals and edicts grow various behaviors and customs, like going to church, attending Bible studies, and relishing religiously inflected holidays like Christmas and Hanukkah. Religion is something around which people bond and create communities. It's a catalyst for connection. Since human beings are a social species, the ideas that have best allowed for people to remain in tightly knit groups are more beneficial for the propagation of the species. Despite the fact that many religions contain principles now considered out of step with contemporary values, they continue to espouse a sense of unity among practitioners that outshines virtually every other.

The ideas make sense on paper, but how, you might be wondering, does all of this talk of religion extend to the Marvel Cinematic Universe? This universe is composed of numerous characters that connect to form a single, collective storyline, and fans devote their lives to studying and enjoying these narratives.

Marvel's characters, however relatable on a human level, are essentially gods with superhuman abilities, something scholar and Georgia College professor Mary Magoulick singles out as a defining trait of virtually all myths.[160] On a more practical level, almost every religion has a church or Mecca. For Marvel fans, it's the convention scene.

Every year, dozens of cities across the country, across the world, draw swarms of people dressed head to toe in costumes, memorabilia, and just a dash of eccentricity—fans who have devoted some portion of their lives to loving certain characters, series, and contemporary mythologies.[161] The 2018 San Diego Comic-Con drew more than 130,000 people, and that was only in one city! Historically, these conventions have been seen as virtually a different planet, teeming with that most curious of creatures: the geek. For people who have felt isolated because of their nichey hobbies, these conventions are some of the only places they can truly, comfortably be themselves. Now, in a world where the MCU is the single-highest-grossing franchise in cinema history, it's officially hip to be square.

But you don't need to look to Comic-Con to find the church of Marvel. Just zip to your nearest multiplex. When *Black Panther* was released, it was celebrated for featuring a predominantly Black cast driving a tent-pole blockbuster. Viewers showed up in droves—a quick surf through the Internet will reveal a photographic goldmine of people dressed in traditional African wardrobes of the boldest colors, with some even rocking beaded dashikis to punctuate their enthusiasm in ceremonial fashion.

Before there is too much skepticism, this is not to claim that we'll all be attending the formal church of *Captain America* within the next twenty years. Unlike many other mythologies, the storylines of these comic book characters don't purport to explain how the universe works on a natural, mechanical level the way Greek and Roman mythologies did in fantastical ways. But it says quite a bit that one of the primary characters in the biggest movie franchise ever is literally a Norse god. And although we may not have a church of Cap', the character is a vehicle for values that unite people in enormous numbers, with *Captain America: Civil War* (2016) bringing in grosses that passed the $1 billion mark internationally. In a world as advanced as ours, maybe veneration of superheroes is the next natural step.

After a massive survey was conducted across three years and twelve countries, results published in the *Guardian* showed that 70 percent of youths in the United Kingdom between the ages of sixteen and twenty-nine identified as nonreligious, with 59 percent of surveyed UK youths saying they didn't attend any kind of religious gathering.[162] In the US, the results are just as shocking. The General Social Survey states that the percentage of citizens identifying as nonreligious has increased from 8 percent to 23 percent from 1990 to 2019.[163] According to a piece by Allen Downey published on *Scientific American*'s website, by 2030, a third of Americans are predicted to identify as having no religious preference whatsoever.[164] Perhaps the movie theater is turning into the born-again church of a whole new century after all. Perhaps it already has. Here's what can be said: in a world where religion is a source of devastating ideological divide, uniting under an affection for comic book heroes with unbending standards of justice and equality doesn't sound like the most unappealing idea.

Chapter 10

DAVID AND GOLIATH

Earlier in this book, we talked about the influence of Frank Capra. Here we'll discuss a slew of filmmakers who followed in the footsteps of his characters, taking their ideals to the front steps of the establishment and shouting them from the rooftops to world-shattering effect. The difference is that they're real.

Too many people feel powerless, too small to escape the overwhelming shadows of the issues they face every day. But history has proven with greater and greater frequency that one person is all it takes to start a movement that can cause landslide change—especially in the medium of documentary.

Michael Moore

Within the crowded arena of social impact documentary filmmaking, there's rarely a louder and more ferocious voice than that of Michael Moore. Some would argue that's not necessarily a good thing—Moore is known for his confrontational tactics that err more on the side of showmanship than empathy-driven introspection, but if you need someone to go to bat for you in the marketplace of ideas, Michael Moore's ruthless pursuit to provoke and make change is maybe the best tool to have on your side.

Moore's filmmaking has covered topics from capitalism (in 2009's *Capitalism: A Love Story*) to the George W. Bush administration's handling of the 2001 terrorist attacks in *Fahrenheit 9/11* (2004). Far from the observational poetry of a documentarian like Werner Herzog, Moore's films place him at the center of the action, going from place to place, subject to subject, often veiling his anarchic motivations with put-on coyness—for example, he shows up to high-security buildings asking to speak with high-profile individuals, pretending not to understand why they might not want to talk to him, given that they're the ones he's trying to skewer. And *skewer* is the right word. His films are assembled with the shot-by-shot efficiency of a military-grade weapon, and they're just as loud, just as piercing.

Michael Moore was born in 1954 in the industry-rich flatlands of Flint, Michigan, and his passions in youth were, perhaps, surprising to nobody, more rooted in the world of journalism than out-and-out filmmaking. After high school, Moore devoted much of his focus toward confronting American injustice, dropping out of college after a year to find an outlet for his voice by founding the underground newspaper the *Michigan Voice*; he would stay with the paper for more than ten years, serving as an editor. There, he would sharpen his craft and cultivate the feather-ruffling tendencies that have made him equally famous and infamous.

Moore's typical middle-American upbringing didn't fit the mold for the left-wing radical iconoclast he's become. Moore attended Catholic schools until high school and even spent some years devoted to the Boy Scouts, however strange it might be to imagine Moore belonging to an organization so stratified. But on his father's side, Moore's connections to his political outrage are more clear—his dad worked in an automobile-assembly factory in the heart of the city's main industry. It's easy to feel, therefore, the personal connection to his hometown and the auto industry, and when the 1980s uprooted the industrial focus that was the bread and butter of the city's working-class income, Moore didn't just take the issue personally—he took it into his hands, dissected it, and displayed it for the world to behold.

This is his 1989 debut feature documentary, *Roger & Me*, which regularly appears on critic roundups of the most acclaimed documentaries of all time. It showcases the people and culture of Flint, Michigan, the birthplace of General Motors. During his opening narration, Moore recounts how three generations of his family worked in the factories—automobile manufacturing has been as central to Flint's industry and well-being as it has been to the working-class populace of Detroit.

At the time of the film's release, General Motors was achieving record profits that carved the company's place among the biggest automobile makers in the world. Why, then, were nearly thirty thousand Flint auto workers laid off, causing what Moore argued was a partial economic collapse of the entire community? It's this note that adds a sense of the prodigal son to Moore's journey—his goal was always to leave Flint and make a name for himself, but there's an unspoken sense that just as he moved away from Flint, so, too, did corporate America. Did he feel some responsibility, therefore, to return to his old stomping ground to fight on Flint's behalf?

What is difficult to understand is how completely—if Moore's portrait is to be believed—the affluent stratum of Flint abandoned its middle and lower classes. He interviews the rich at country clubs, golf courses, fundraisers, spare-no-expense luncheons, and flex-my-cash-athons at which all people in attendance seem totally oblivious to the realities of working-class Flint citizens. They don't realize that some people's entire skill set has been eliminated for purely corporate gains. Some even go on camera and accuse people experiencing financial hardship of being too negative, too lazy, to pick themselves up and search for other work. These are people like GM CEO Roger Smith, with whom Moore persistently tries to meet to confront him over the reality of his decision to lay off Flint workers. Meanwhile, we see Moore interview a lady whose husband was laid off during the industrial closure and now resorts to illegally raising rabbits for pets and meat—in one of the more horrifying sequences, we watch her smash a rabbit's head, behead it, and then skin it, all to make money for groceries.

Stories like this are intercut with Moore following around an eviction agent throwing people out of their homes. The agent stops every few instances to explain himself to the camera: "It's a job," he keeps saying. Everyone from single mothers to people Moore knew from high school are put out on the street. All the evictions paint a larger picture: the laying off of Flint auto workers didn't impact just their individual lives but the economy of the area as a whole. At the film's beginning, Moore's camera shows a vibrant Flint, full of life, vigor, and community. Over the three years Moore filmed the documentary, we see it change to a hopeless wasteland of financial struggle. And by the time he finally gets a chance to confront Roger Smith, the CEO is completely indifferent, too busy celebrating Christmas to care about the people losing their homes on the same holiday.

But the film that catapulted Moore to the status of household name, and the one that had some noticeable real-world impact, was far more controversial, and far more influential than *Roger & Me*: the searing 2002 indictment of American gun culture, *Bowling for Columbine*. The movie opens in a way that is quintessentially Moore: he walks into a bank, uses his everyman charm to endear himself both to bank employees and the audience, and opens up a special bank account that gives him a free gun. It seems absolutely absurd, but sure enough, he walks out wielding a full-on, high-grade rifle that was given to him like the prize in a box of Cracker Jack by the bank employees themselves. The ease of attainment is part of the film's compelling thesis: America loves guns, but more importantly, there's a political and financial incentive to make us feel that we need them for our protection.

The film is less an attack on guns—Moore admits on camera that he's a card-carrying member of the National Rifle Association—than a criticism of what he considers a culture of fear engendered by American media and the powerful voices of biased politicians. The Columbine High School massacre in 1999 is more a centerpiece on the table of conversation than a subject scrutinized in detail. It's one of many examples of gun violence that could have been certainly prevented with shifts in cultural attitudes. Interviewed are fellow cultural transgressors like Matt Stone, cocreator of *South Park*, and maestro of the musical macabre, Marilyn Manson—an easy scapegoat for Columbine after it was discovered that the shooters, Dylan Klebold and Eric Harris, were avid fans of his music.

Whatever your perspective on gun ownership, the case Moore slowly but emphatically builds is an enormously compelling one. In its most moving and disturbing section, Moore creates a montage over which Louis Armstrong's "What a Wonderful World" plays to blood-curdling effect. He constructs a timeline of events in which the United States essentially builds an international network of political violence and weapons trade culminating in the 9/11 terrorist attacks, an event Moore implicitly argues we indirectly funded and empowered.

As a piece of filmmaking, *Bowling for Columbine* roars like a Mack truck and pulses with a newborn's heart, painting a picture of all-encompassing gun culture so stomach-churning, the audience feels complicit in the damage done on-screen. And despite Moore's approaching his ideas with sledgehammer subtlety, the film is also incredibly multifaceted, analyzing a complicated issue from a variety of angles, each with its own part to play in the bigger picture. For example, Moore holds the media responsible for relying on the "if it bleeds, it leads" angle—or in other words, fear-based programming—to the point of traumatizing its audience. If you watch the news regularly, he argues, you'll start to think everybody including the babysitter is out to kill you when you least expect it.

The film's gut punch, however, also proves to be one of its most triumphant accomplishments: Michael Moore employs the help of the Columbine victims, two of whom still have bullets from that terrifying day lodged in their bodies, to force a confrontation that's one of Michael Moore's favorite tactics: coyly asking questions in ways that won't make those on the receiving end look anything but villainous. Moore and the kids visit Kmart's headquarters in Troy, Michigan, to ask for a refund based on the damage done to them by the bullets the superstore juggernaut sold. At that time, automatic weapons and their ammunition were sold over the counter—anybody, in theory, could waltz in and buy an infinite amount. When confronted by the kids, the Kmart PR and communications team is at first stunned. The end result is an on-camera victory most activists could only dream of: as a result of the students' impassioned plea, Kmart agrees to phase out the availability of ammunition for consumer firearms.

The final interview of the film, and indeed a cringeworthy coda to all the proceedings, is a confrontation with an aging Charlton Heston, actor of *Ben-Hur* fame as well as then-president of the National Rifle Association. Moore asks Heston why gun violence is such a problem in the US and why he held an NRA rally in Denver, Colorado, after the school massacre at Columbine, just ten miles away. When Moore further requests Heston's apology for appearing in Flint, Michigan, for an NRA rally following the shooting of a six-year-old girl by a six-year-old boy at a local school, Heston abruptly ends the interview and walks out without ever arriving at an explanation or a sound line of reasoning, underlining the contradictions and gung-ho tunnel vision surrounding gun policies in the US.

You may not agree with what Michael Moore has to say. You may even think he's a morally unscrupulous asshole who yells far more than he should, but at the end of the day, Michael Moore's goal is never to be agreed with or, indeed, to be liked: it's to be heard, and beyond rhetoric and grandstanding, Michael Moore is never easily forgotten. He's brash, he's biased, and he's proudly unsubtle. And in the case of *Bowling for Columbine*, he was the catalyst for a series of changes that may very well have saved lives. If that's the effect a documentary can have, we need a lot more like them—especially given that gun violence in the US has risen to such unprecedented heights that, according CBS News, mass shootings in which more than four people at a time are wounded or killed occur more than once a day.[165]

Super Size Me

Born in West Virginia, Morgan Spurlock attended New York University's Tisch School of the Arts, graduating in 1993. Although he spent his college years cultivating his interest in cinema, he initially started his career as a writer and playwright, garnering awards from both the New York International Fringe Festival and the Route 66 American Playwriting Competition for his play *The Phoenix*. Throughout the 1990s, Spurlock balanced these early writing endeavors with miscellaneous work in the New York film scene, with uncredited work as a production assistant on Woody Allen's *Bullets over Broadway* and the Nicolas Cage thriller *Kiss of Death*, and, perhaps most worthy of note, credited work as an assistant on Luc Besson's classic crime thriller *Léon: The Professional*.

It wasn't until a few years later that Spurlock would have his first encounter with the world of television. He began an Internet series called *I Bet You Will*, composed of five-to-ten-minute episodes of random participants presented as "normal" people who were involved in variously outrageous stunts for cash rewards. This included feats such as eating an entire jar of mayonnaise in one sitting and throwing back shot glasses filled with increasingly nauseating ingredients, including Pepto-Bismol, hot sauce, corn oil, and cod-liver oil. If the contestant resisted, unsatisfied with the cash reward tethered to the stunt, Spurlock and cohost Willa Ford tended to raise the reward until they won over the contestant, proving that virtually everybody has a price—thus the title, *I Bet You Will*. The series gained so much steam that it attracted the attention of multimedia titan MTV, who picked it up and turned it into a full-fledged series of thirty-minute episodes.

These were tastes of success, flirtations with it. But it wasn't until 2004 that Spurlock would launch himself into the stratosphere with a documentary called *Super Size Me*, a scathing indictment of the fast-food industry that scorched the Earth even as it swept it.

Spurlock was inspired by a 2002 story of a nineteen-year-old and a fourteen-year-old who were suing fast-food juggernaut McDonald's for health problems linked to their obesity. Jazlyn Bradley and Ashley Pelman both ate meals from McDonald's several days a week and usually more than one meal per day. Bradley was five-foot-six and weighed 270 pounds; Pelman was four-foot-ten and clocked in at 170. The teenage plaintiffs claimed that McDonald's did not provide any information pertaining to the nutritional value or health risks of the food they served and that they were therefore responsible for the young girls' declining physical health. The story was sensational, appearing in outlets from the *New York Times* to the *Guardian*. The case struck a chord with a national crisis: America wasn't just fat but seemingly getting fatter by the day, with 61 percent of adults and 14 percent of adolescents qualifying as overweight in 1999.[166]

The courts eventually struck down the young girls' claims, citing personal responsibility, common sense, and the lack of direct evidence that it was McDonald's specifically that seeded their ailments. All reasonable points, certainly, but in the fashion of lawyers, the court sadly dodged far more pressing questions than anybody had the stomach to answer—pun not intended. If McDonald's wasn't to blame, did blame solely rest on the girls? And more importantly, what was to be done to prevent the Land of the Free from smothering in its own flesh and dietary self-indulgence?

Since a lack of evidence sealed the case, Spurlock took it upon himself to provide some. He figured that if he could prove using his own body that eating a regular diet of McDonald's food could have drastic and immediate impact on one's health, that would blow the blame-game defense wide open. Although Bradley and Pelman had lost their case in court, perhaps the court of public opinion would suffice. To accomplish this, Spurlock established a rigorous eating scheme: he had to order three meals a day from McDonald's for thirty days straight; he had to order every item on the menu at least one time during the course of the experiment; if the employees asked him if he wanted to "Supersize" his meal, he had to say yes—but he could Supersize it only if they asked; and he committed to walking the surveyed national average of five thousand steps a day. As part of the experiment, he worked with a trio of physicians—a gastroenterologist, a cardiologist, and a general practitioner—along with a dietician and a personal trainer, to administer routine checkups and recommendations, not only to ensure that all changes in health were carefully measured and documented but also to keep Spurlock aware of how much, and how exactly, he was putting himself at risk.

Spurlock did all of the above. He ate three meals a day—pancakes or an Egg McMuffin in the morning and chicken sandwich, Filet-O-Fish, or Big Mac and crispy golden French fries for lunch or dinner. At the very beginning, Spurlock is virtually an item of envy, gorging on every fast-food delight with the kind of relish one could expect from a six-year-old. But then things begin to change. When Spurlock is sprung with his first Supersize meal—featuring a Double Quarter Pounder with Cheese, nearly a half pound of fries, and a third of a gallon of Coca-Cola—he throws his head out the window launching more amber-colored spew than you could imagine coming from something as simple as a drive-through burger meal. Clearly his body was beginning to fight back.

Yet this continued, escalating with each new circle of fast-food Hell. Weight gain was inevitable. What shocked Spurlock and doctors alike were the mood swings, night sweats, depression, and addictive symptoms he developed the more McDonalds he ate. The trials were at once frightening, nauseating, and, strangest of all, funny, with each new bite of burger taking on a greater sense of tightrope-caliber risk that Spurlock seemed committed to overcoming. And for the most part, it worked. By taking full command of his accessible, everyman persona, Spurlock turned what could have been a rather tedious exercise in watching someone eat themselves to death into a genuine journey of perseverance. The audience laughed along with him at the absurdity of the entire endeavor. (There's a memorable moment a few days into the experiment where he acknowledged that for the first time, he bought a burger that somewhat resembled the polished Big Macs in the pictures and ads.) He also regularly featured his then-girlfriend, Alex Jamieson, a renowned holistic foods chef and diet coach. At the time the film was being shot, Alex was a strict vegan, and the majority of Spurlock's antics left her at either an eye-rolling loss or a terrified gasp.

Along with the experiment on his own body, Spurlock embarked on a cross-country exploration of America's relationship with fast food. Most significant are his interviews at schools to examine the ways poor meal choices can impact students' behavior and academic performance. Responding to Bradley and Pelman's claims against McDonald's that nutritional information was not readily available, Spurlock again dives in. He visits dozens of McDonald's locations throughout New York City, only to find the nutritional information is either misleading, discreetly located, or out-and-out unavailable—many locations are completely out of the proper pamphlets to educate customers about the food they're consuming.

The journey also reveals how people sometimes have a deeper connection to fast food than other cultural artifacts that are arguably more substantial. Spurlock conducts an interview with a family, all overweight to varying degrees, as they make at least three attempts to recite the national anthem. None are successful. Immediately after, Spurlock asks them to recite the Big Mac slogan. They nail it. In another example that's even more alarming, Spurlock interviews a selection of young schoolchildren, showing them pictures of various pop culture icons and historical figures, including presidents and even Jesus. Given their relative immaturity, it's no shock that they don't know all of them. But when he shows them Ronald McDonald and the Wendy's mascot, they all experience a stark moment of clarity and shout out the names.

The thirty-day experiment produced results frightening and shocking.[167] By the time he'd had his last round of doctor's visits, Morgan Spurlock had gained more than twenty-four pounds, giving him a massive gut within 30 days; to the surprise of nobody, his cholesterol skyrocketed; he'd nearly doubled his chances for heart disease and rapidly increased the levels of uric acid polluting his system, setting the stage for gout to settle in; his liver had begun to leak enzymes, which is one of the red flags for a failing liver; and by any medical definition, Spurlock had become addicted to the food he'd been eating the past four weeks.[168] If Spurlock hadn't quite pushed himself to the point of death, the biological arrangements were clearly being made. Had he gone on longer with the experiment, his body would have been permanently damaged, and heart disease would be inevitable.

Criticism of the film was almost immediate, and often as heated as the outrage the film sparked toward the industry it criticized. While some viewers raved about the film, claiming it stoked crucial fires few other voices were courageous enough to tackle, other audience members were skeptical, picking out holes in Spurlock's presentation. For example, who on Earth eats McDonald's three meals a day? Who orders an ice cream sundae or a milkshake every day? To some, pointing to these habits as evidence that fast food could kill you was akin to saying that drinking three gallons of water every day could kill you. What did it prove beyond the dangers of overconsumption? In the wake of the film's success, there were several articles and even feature-length documentaries in their own right that attempted to disprove Spurlock's findings, the most notable of which was comedian Tom Naughton's film *Fat Head* (2009). A lady named Soso Whaley even claimed she'd lost eighteen pounds and *lowered* her cholesterol by a staggering forty points by adhering to a comparable McDonald's diet.

Spurlock was undeterred—validated, even. The point of making a documentary isn't necessarily to tell nothing but the clean-cut truth, but rather to incite conversations about issues certain people would rather brush beneath the cultural rug. If people were criticizing the film, it meant that people were thinking about it, asking questions, performing investigations, and informing themselves in ways they might not have otherwise.

Those questions scared the right people. Within six weeks of the release of *Super Size Me*, McDonald's removed Supersize portions from all of its menus. If Spurlock's findings were so outlandish and unfounded, why would an international corporation as mammoth as McDonald's change its menus worldwide? If the truth was truly in their favor, why not allow it to speak for itself? Perhaps the truth did speak volumes. And that was precisely McDonald's fear. Aside from becoming a word-of-mouth sensation, Spurlock and company were nominated for Best Documentary at the 2005 Academy Awards, and although they lost out on the big night in favor of a film on the Indian sex trade called *Born into Brothels*, the Oscar nomination cemented the movie's presence in the arena of cultural discourse.

While it's been well over a decade since the film's release, and Spurlock himself has been immersed in scandal as a result of sexual misconduct and alcoholism, McDonald's continues to do damage control to this day, rebranding again and again as health-conscious and transparent about the nutritional value of what does and does not go into its food.

Errol Morris and the Thin Blue Line

Of all the examples of filmmakers confronting the impenetrable walls of the institution—in this case the American judicial system—*The Thin Blue Line* (1988) is perhaps the most inspirational, and inarguably a watershed moment in the history of documentary filmmaking. The whiz behind the film, Errol Morris, is considered less of a conventional documentarian than a sort of investigative intellectual—he doesn't just try to find the truth but rather examines, film by film, its very nature as a concept.

Born in the suburbs of Hewlett, New York, Errol Morris continues the pattern of great filmmakers coming from less-than-cinematic origins. His fledgling fascinations weren't necessarily with cinema but with history and philosophy, and he spent his college years building up to a bachelor's degree in history from the University of Wisconsin–Madison. But it was his time at Princeton for graduate work that would produce one of his defining moments, an encounter that not only ignited the intellectual spark in him but exemplified the hard line he would take in the name of truth for the rest of his career.

Somehow, through conversational sleight of hand, Morris managed to sneak his way into a seminar by none other than Thomas Kuhn, the philosopher of science behind the groundbreaking book *The Structure of Scientific Revolutions*. As recounted in an autobiographical piece for the *New York Times*, while Morris sat through the lecture, listening to Kuhn regale his students about the relativism around reality, he began to notice that Kuhn's ideas directly clashed with his own more material philosophy that truth is objective and rooted. Being the curious mind that he was, he voiced his objections to what he considered Kuhn's nihilism. Kuhn pushed back, and Morris claims that the back-and-forth became so heated that Kuhn threw a glass ashtray full of cigarette butts at Morris's head.[169]

We can't know if this is what inspired Morris to drop out of graduate school, but one thing was certain: Morris was blazing his own path, and he decided to pursue it straight to filmmaking. When he wasn't making critically hailed darlings like *Gates of Heaven*, Morris was paying his bills as a private detective in the '80s, solving various cases and sharpening his wits and métier for the truth.[170] This experience cemented the staunchness of his perception—in an interview with Ron Rosenbaum of *Smithsonian* magazine, he says, "I'm amazed that you still see this nonsense all over the place, that truth is relative, that truth is subjective. People still cling to it."[171]

Errol Morris is known for his meticulously constructed documentaries about enigmatic people and situations—just watch *Tabloid* (2010) to witness a filmmaker approach an inane story objectively. But *The Thin Blue Line* (1988), his most acclaimed film, did more than explore a complicated criminal charge; it played a vital role in saving a man from serving a life sentence in prison on false charges.

A film is nothing without its subject, and *The Thin Blue Line* is a many-layered labyrinth of tragedy and deceit, all starting with one night in 1976.

That morning, twenty-seven-year-old Randall Dale Adams was a completely different person living a completely different life. He was a high school graduate and former US Army paratrooper born the youngest of five children in Grove City, Ohio. By even the kindest standards, his life was mundane, perhaps even pleasantly so. Adams was on a road trip to California with his brother when they made a fateful stop in Texas. After being offered a job, Adams decided to stay and pursue the opportunity. While in Texas one night, driving along the highway, Adams's car broke down. A sixteen-year-old boy named David Ray Harris stopped to ask if Adams needed any help. Adams accepted the ride from Harris and found, over the course of several hours, that they enjoyed each other's company and really clicked—they drank, smoked, and reveled in the heedlessness of youth before parting ways at the end of the night.

This sounds like the very best version of a road movie, where everything is possible given the right intersection of circumstances. Except one thing: what Adams didn't know when they parted ways was that the car David Ray Harris was driving had been stolen. The very next day, Harris was stopped on the highway by patrolman Robert Wood for driving with no headlights. As the officer walked toward the vehicle, Harris shot him twice, once in forearm and once in the chest. Wood's partner, patrol officer Teresa Turko, fired several shots as Harris sped away, but she missed. Later on, in an effort to avoid his own arrest, Harris claimed that Randall Adams had committed the crime and that Harris had simply been present in the car at the time.

Adams was taken in for questioning, and despite complying with every step of the process, he managed to fail his polygraph. Harris, on the other hand, passed his with flying colors. Who knows why? Perhaps Adams got nervous, intimidated by the intense questioning by the authorities—cops have a tendency to do that, especially to young working-class men from out of town. The bottom line: Adams was in dire straits, and the law was no longer on his side. In the eyes of the police, he had murdered a cop and fled the scene of the crime, and he would be punished with maximum severity.

When Adams was tried, Turko identified the assailant as having the same hair color as Adams, despite admitting that she'd never gotten a clear view of his face. That was enough for the jury. In a horrifying turn of events, the jury found Adams guilty of murder, and he was subsequently slated for the death penalty. The strange part was that at that time, the death penalty could be used in sentencing only if a psychiatrist had dubbed the defendant not only guilty but also unrepentant and an incurable menace to society. Eventually, Adams's death sentence was commuted to life in prison—the only glimmer of hope he saw for twelve years.

But wait just one moment. The plot thickens, and the tale becomes even stranger as a man named Errol Morris enters the frame. At that time, Morris was still in the budding stages of his lauded filmmaking career, having just hit the scene with a pair of groundbreaking documentaries, the essential-viewing *Gates of Heaven* and its semisequel *Vernon, Florida*. Errol was in search of a new project, one that would allow him to probe further depths, so he turned to infamous criminal psychiatrist James Grigson, nicknamed Dr. Death for his seemingly unyielding commitment to testifying in favor of the maximum possible sentence. Over Grigson's storied career, he testified in more than 167 capital cases, and virtually all of them resulted in the death penalty. As Errol Morris was prepping his in-depth look into the mind of such a prolific hands-off executioner, he learned that Grigson had testified during the Adams murder trial—a chain of events he had long been fascinated by. So rather than narrowing his scope to one man, his field of interest soon pivoted to the whole case. He conducted extensive research and came to the conclusion that's hopefully obvious: something, albeit who knew what exactly, was not right.

Morris compiled hours upon hours of interviews with everybody involved in the case, including Randall Dale Adams. The conversations reveal that Adams is a calm, unassuming, and utterly casual man—there is no doubt in his mind that he's innocent, but he doesn't speak with the passionate confidence of a framed man. His eyes are vacant, perhaps after years of being worn down by the reality of his cell walls.

Combined with these interviews is a series of staged reenactments of various descriptions of the events as told by members of the defense and prosecution teams. Over the course of the documentary's brisk one and a half hours, the information is presented piece by careful piece, taking great care to provide as many perspectives as possible without bogging down the viewer. An important discovery is made in this meticulous process: after engineering Adams's conviction for the murder he himself committed, Harris was slammed on one burglary charge after another spanning several states. In 1985 he broke into a Texas apartment, attempted to abduct a woman, and shot her boyfriend, Mark Mays, to death.

All of this information is deployed quietly and carefully, never resorting to easy gimmes, pulled heartstrings, or even the kind of rabble-rousing grandstanding that Michael Moore might use with the same material. Morris isn't attempting to bang his audience over the head with politics or agenda but rather to slyly expose the other side of a story most of the people involved would rather have kept hidden. By the end of the film, it's clear that Harris was lying, leaving the audience with a revelation as delicately played as it is deeply unsettling: sometimes the democratic justice system we so heavily rely upon and adore truly does fail the people who need it most.

The film was a bombshell upon release, flaying the skin from a legal process toward which a significant percentage of laypeople have a certain degree of blind faith. Despite the film's not being nominated for an Academy Award on what was ultimately a technicality, audiences were astounded by the revelations the movie delivered so effectively. So loud was the acclaim and so fiery was the buzz around the film that something unprecedented happened: in the months following the film's release, authorities reopened

Randall Adams's case. Adams was even set to be released on bond, and when an opposing prosecutor tried to have the bond raised to one hundred thousand dollars in cash, Errol Morris himself offered to split the difference, essentially paying for Adams's freedom. Fortunately, that drastic measure wasn't necessary: after arguing against the prosecution's case, the district court judge restored the bond to its original terms, and Adams was released. In the end, Adams's sentence was overturned, and he was permitted to leave prison after serving twelve years of his life sentence.

Harris was eventually convicted and put to death for the murder of Mark Mays, but he was never prosecuted for the murder of the patrol officer that he had pinned on Adams. Furthermore, seven years after the film was released, the infamous "Dr. Death" was expelled from the American Psychiatric Association for "arriving at a psychiatric diagnosis without first having examined the individuals in question, and for indicating, while testifying in court as an expert witness, that he could predict with 100 percent certainty that the individuals would engage in future violent acts."[172]

Errol Morris went on to explore a number of equally fascinating and singular subjects in films including *The Unknown Known* (2013), exploring the career and political foibles of Donald Rumsfeld; *Tabloid* (2010), the bizarre story of a kidnapping that turned into the sexual exploits between a young Mormon missionary and a North Carolina woman, capturing the nation before descending into disturbing levels of strangeness; and *A Brief History of Time* (1991), arguably the definitive documentary on Stephen Hawking, the late physicist who revolutionized black hole physics from the confines of a wheelchair.

Morris is widely considered a master of documentary

filmmaking. His crime scene recreations in *The Thin Blue Line* have been mimicked and rebuilt many times since the film's release in 1988. But more importantly, he stands as a testament to the power of filmmaking; if he hadn't made this film, Randall Adams might very well have rotted in jail until his untimely death at sixty-one from a brain tumor. But thanks to Morris, his last twenty-one years were spent in the freedom that he had been deprived of by law.

Despite *The Thin Blue Line* being one of the most acclaimed documentaries of all time, Morris expressed disappointment that he'd lost the money he'd put into it and that he and Adams ended up in a dispute about who owned what rights to the story. In a larger perspective, was it worth it? If *The Thin Blue Line* proves anything, it's that films don't just inform or entertain. At their most potent and impactful, they can literally save lives.

Chapter 11

STORYTELLING AND EDUCATION

There was a time in history when the idea of teaching people through a television set was not simply a ridiculous idea but a borderline-offensive one. Remember when you were a child, and you were told that watching too much television would turn your eyes square? Who knows where this rumor started. Was television looked down upon because of the threat it posed to theatrical cinema? Perhaps. Was the image of families gathered around a machine feeding information to stone-still observers too Orwellian to ever fully sit well in the public consciousness? That's also likely. The bottom line is that somewhere along its evolution, television became vilified as an agent of laziness and moral corruption. To this day, there are people who believe there's something about television that is inherently bad for you, numbing your senses and turning your cognitive faculties into jelly.

But the opposite couldn't be more true. For decades, television has been a medium that has informed the public rather than dumbing it down, reporting current events, dissecting complicated issues, and using entertainment to put a finger on the world's cultural pulse. Because it's such a draw for children—has there ever been a better babysitter when playtime has to be cut short—it's an unparalleled opportunity to introduce young minds to constructive skills like counting, understanding social cues, and even accepting people without judgment. The truth is that the power of television is profound.

Sesame Street

The Muppets, in their original comedic styling fashioned by Jim Henson and company, were so endearingly innocent that it was almost inevitable they'd evolve into tools to teach the youth of the world. It helps that puppets are also entertaining, especially those who are operated by the pros and take on a life of their own. Learning math isn't the greatest amusement to most children (unless they're named Julian Schwinger), but what if the numbers are vocalized by a velvet Dracula complete with thick Transylvanian accent? The medicine simply goes down far more easily—all the way down to nearly two hundred Emmy Awards, in fact. For the fifty years it's been on the air, *Sesame Street* has been one of the most consistently popular and acclaimed children's series of all time.

Since it is one of the crowning achievements in children's television, it's more than fitting that *Sesame Street*'s inspiration came from a child. In the mid-1960s, producer Joan Ganz Cooney was known for furthering the grand tradition of lavish dinner parties, where professionals of various industries could mingle and merge minds and passions. During one such party, a man named Dr. Lloyd Morrisett told Cooney that his daughter was enraptured by television as a technical wonder, sometimes waking up in a quiet house just to switch it on and watch the empty signal fizzle on the screen.

Morrisett was a renowned research psychologist working in the field of childhood education. During his tenure at the Carnegie Corporation, a nonprofit organization promoting learning and education, Morrisett worked with fellow researchers to determine whether or not children who struggled in school would be aided by earlier outreach. The prevailing answer was yes.

Morrisett's casual conversation with Cooney would eventually evolve into more than 4,500 episodes of world-changing collaboration. The two discussed using children's programming as a delivery system to educate less privileged youngsters in less affluent regions who couldn't afford preschool. Together, Morrisett and Cooney assembled a new organization, the Children's Television Workshop (now called the Sesame Workshop), to create this new working experiment.

In the name of science and journalistic integrity, I boldly braved an episode from 2009. It opens with a live-action montage of children interacting with a pink puppet in a real-world setting, as if serving as a vestibule between the world of the viewer and the world of *Sesame Street*. Then the show introduces you to the characters of *Sesame Street*—Grover, Big Bird, Oscar the Grouch, and several others that will charm young newcomers as well as the sentimental hearts of adult children—before breaking down into self-contained segments, some live action and others animated. Each segment focuses on one set of characters, akin to a different "house" along the stretches of *Sesame Street*.

In the episode I watched, Big Bird finds the autumnal climate of *Sesame Street* too cold and unfit for a bird. This catches the attention of real-estate agent Freddy Flapman, played in early glory by Lin-Manuel Miranda of *Hamilton* fame, who attempts to convince Big Bird that perhaps another environment would make him feel more at home. After all, birds don't belong in cities during the winter. But as the conversation continues, we realize that

Flapman hopes to get Big Bird to move only to make a real-estate sale, which is why it's such a relief that the big yellow bird doesn't ultimately fall for his scheme. In the end, Big Bird realizes that his home is wherever his friends are, and that if he's to live anywhere, *Sesame Street* is the perfect residence for a bird like him.

There's something quietly revelatory about a segment this simple. It triples in purpose as an opportunity to explain the migration habits of birds, a comprehensive introduction to the concept of a habitat, and an exploration of the varieties of environments in which birds and animals thrive. By the end, it's also a fable about feeling comfortable precisely where you are, even if other people attempt to convince you otherwise. After all, children are often subject to peer pressure, a phenomenon that can create vicious cycles into adulthood if they don't learn to resist it early in life.

According to a 2015 report by the US Department of Education, only 40 percent of four-year-olds across the United States are enrolled in some kind of publicly funded preschool program.[173] That means 60 percent of children aren't receiving the kind of head start that would prepare them for elementary school. This is not to suggest that any of these children won't see success later in life, but it doesn't take a statistician to understand that the earlier you have experiences with worldly skills, the more of an advantage you'll have when you get started in the classroom. These kids begin school without the kinds of basic skills—counting, colors, the alphabet, healthy eating habits—that the other 40 percent of children are gifted. Or, at least, they would lack these skills were it not for *Sesame Street*.

What kind of real-world effect did *Sesame Street* have on its viewers? Seeking to answer this question, the Educational Testing Service

(ETS) reviewed a series of sixteen research studies conducted from 1969 to 1989.[174] In one of these studies, called the Age Cohort Study, conducted in the late '60s and early '70s, researchers selected two groups of children aged fifty-three to fifty-eight months (between four and five years old). A control group that lacked exposure to *Sesame Street* was compiled from test scores recorded in 1969, before *Sesame Street* had graced the airwaves. The study found that the children who had seen *Sesame Street* consistently scored higher than kids who hadn't.[175] This data may not provide definitive proof, but it's a great foundation in favor of *Sesame Street*'s case. To double down on that observed trend, in a separate-but-similar experiment conducted in Australia in 1971, only one child with no exposure to *Sesame Street* scored higher than the children who had watched the show.[176] There's always an outlier.

A 1972 study detailed in the ETS report also showed encouraging results. Researchers compared children from two different day-care centers, one of which regularly screened *Sesame Street* while the other did so with significantly less frequency. Each group of children took part in a series of exercises: first naming letters of the alphabet in groups of four, then naming geometric figures. When looking at the results, it was the children who had had exposure to *Sesame Street* who excelled.[177]

The ETS report itself confesses that the series of studies is something of a mixed bag, with individual results cobbled together from preexisting data or data that was obtained through methodologically incomplete means. But combing all sixteen studies creates a collective narrative that nevertheless tells the same story in different ways: in all but one of the studies, *Sesame Street* had an observable positive impact on the comprehension and abilities of children.[178]

In the mid-2010s, *Sesame Street* began to change in ways that might have put rocks in the stomachs of people who were raised on the show. It moved from its nearly half-century home of PBS to the more private network at HBO, and its run time was slashed from an hour to thirty minutes. At first glance, this seems to spell the end for the kind of impact *Sesame Street* can have on its audience. The whole appeal of the series is that PBS costs viewers nothing as long as they have access to a TV, whereas HBO has always been seen as a premium service. But in defense of the decision, as the broadcasting landscape evolves to adapt to the presence of streaming and related innovations, it may be a way to ensure that *Sesame Street* lives on well past the conventional model of free television.

But whether it's HBO, PBS, or a service that will beam episodes of the felt-stitched universe directly to your mobile device, the future all but foretells that *Sesame Street* will always have some sort of home in the American consciousness as it continues to embolden and academically enrich budding generations.

Mister Rogers' Neighborhood

"It's a beautiful day in this neighborhood."[179] And *this neighborhood* is really *every* neighborhood, thanks largely to one man and his squeaky-clean spirit. For several generations of young viewers, hearing those melodic chimes and seeing that scale model of a red trolley rolling through a miniaturized neighborhood meant that no matter what else was happening in the world, a burst of wholesome positivity was within reach.

Fred Rogers, known to the world simply as Mister Rogers, was far more than a television host. He was a lifeboat for those who were facing difficult upbringings, children too young to deal with the complexities of their lives. Mister Rogers used television not only to educate and to entertain but also to provide solace, acceptance, and self-esteem to the people around him, both in front of and behind the cameras. His legacy is love and an emphasis on understanding one's own feelings.

From his unforgettably gentle demeanor to his unorthodox upbringing, Fred Rogers fit the mold of the unlikely hero like a winter glove. He was born into an affluent, devoutly Christian household and lived out his childhood in the Pittsburgh, Pennsylvania, area accordingly. The sensitivity he exuded in his adulthood arose from childhood—he was timid, overweight, not particularly confident, and even sickly—he was often isolated due to being plagued by everything from asthma to scarlet fever. In the documentary *Won't You Be My Neighbor?* (2018), Rogers confesses that much of his childlike sensitivity came from his loneliness. He had to exercise his imagination to keep himself entertained, including inventing his own playmates—playmates that would evolve through adulthood into the characters that populated his acclaimed series.

After Rogers graduated from college in 1951, he had every intention of spending his adult years as a member of the clergy. But then he discovered something that would switch the rails on his entire future: television. To us in the twenty-first century, a household television set is as commonplace as indoor plumbing, but to Rogers in the early '50s, it was practically a thing of science fiction, with information beamed from all over the country and transmitted in fuzzy black and white. He decided that rather than express his Christian values in sermons, he could use television to deliver messages of love, nobility, and grace to thousands of people at once. This idea might seem tame by contemporary standards, but for a man in the '50s, it was practically punk rock.

For someone who would define himself on the small screen, Fred Rogers was notoriously venomous toward television. Not toward the technology, necessarily, but toward how thoughtlessly it was being utilized at the time. He abhorred the nutrition-free wasteland that was children's programming in the early 1950s—polluted with aimless antics and cartoon violence, virtually devoid of anything nurturing. So when the Pittsburgh television station WQED, America's first locally organized and sponsored network for educational programming, connected with Rogers in his post at NBC to help pen their first slate of shows, he immediately sank his teeth into the opportunity. The first program was a simple, low-budget kids' show called *The Children's Corner* that ran from 1955 to 1961. With ramshackle sets and simple host-character interactions, it was a kind of prototype for the series Rogers would pioneer in the '60s. But the show was missing something vital. Though it allowed Rogers to fulfill his goal to connect with children in positive ways, the man himself remained largely behind the scenes. That would change with *Mister Rogers' Neighborhood*.

The series began life in 1961 as a similarly titled series called *Misterogers* on the Canadian Broadcasting Corporation (CBC) network. After living in Toronto for several years to run the show, in 1966 he moved his program to the United States, where it was produced by WQED and distributed regionally by Eastern Educational Network (EEN). Its name was now *Misterogers' Neighborhood*. Within a year, a lack of funding led to the show's cancellation, but in 1968 *Misterogers' Neighborhood* was back with a new influx of cash, this time airing nationwide on National Educational Television (NET), the network that would become the Public Broadcasting Service (PBS).

It seemed almost absurd—how could a lanky, tame, feather-delicate man like Rogers spearhead a widely syndicated TV show? But the network took the risk anyway. And despite some bumps in the road, it paid off, and Fred Rogers quickly became a national phenomenon.

The setup of the show was focused and simple: we begin with a song, "Won't You Be My Neighbor," as Rogers leads us into the world of his house and neighborhood, a safe space where the dangers of the outside are talked about but never lie within harming distance. Then the red trolley transports us from Rogers's house to a land of make-believe, dominated by puppet kings and guest hosts, as a multitude of topics from basic skills to controversial issues are discussed among the characters.

One of history's greatest animators, Don Bluth of *An American Tail* (1986) and *The Secret of NIMH* (1982) fame, once said that as long as you attach a happy ending, children can handle just about any subject matter, regardless of how dark or morose. Nobody invested in that idea more than Fred Rogers. The boldest thing about *Mister Rogers' Neighborhood* was how gracefully the on-screen discussions confronted and digested real-world issues, including everything from the assassination of Robert F. Kennedy to the Vietnam War. In fact, two days after the assassination,[180] Daniel Striped Tiger, one of Rogers's most frequently recurring characters, interrupts a balloon-inflating demonstration to turn to another character, Lady Aberlin, and bashfully ask (voiced by Rogers himself as pure-spiritedly as only he can), "What does *assassination* mean?" The whole show goes dead silent, the melancholia of the moment underlined only by the squeaky release of air from the balloon. The question has the same verbiage and tone as if a child had said it; Mister Rogers is able to provide appropriately phrased answers to harrowing mysteries in a voice that speaks like children and for children. It's a move that would seem controversial even today, but Rogers pulls it off with the same gentle tact he applies to other topics, like bullying or racism.

After several years of national success, Rogers didn't become just an icon—he became synonymous with family values and affectionate catharsis, and he often bridged the gap between conservative delicacy and more progressive social ideas.

The series was also quite often a platform to comfortably transgress the social norms of its era. The beginning of Rogers's television career blossomed in an age where the civil rights movement was everywhere—segregation wasn't universally, legally dismissed until 1964, meaning the airing of Rogers's show overlapped the divide between segregated and integrated America. And the transition was far from smooth. With shifts in social paradigms always come growing pains, and some people held on to their prejudices far into the new millennium. Rogers saw his public platform as a way to help normalize this transition.

In 1968, Rogers incorporated his close friend François Clemmons into the show as the character Officer Clemmons, a friendly, reliable arbiter of justice who just happened to be Black—no mention of his race was ever made.[181] In a move that continues to echo throughout television history, Rogers created a scene in which he, with a smile that shimmers with innocence, soaks his feet in a plastic swimming pool. Officer Clemmons walks into the frame and greets Rogers, who invites him to soak his feet alongside him. There's a moment of reluctance before Clemmons is taken by the moment, removes his boots, and submerges his feet in the same water Rogers occupies. This gesture might not seem like much today, but it bridged the gap between the old world and the new. Not only was Officer Clemmons among the very first recurring Black characters on a children's TV show,[182] the image of two men of different skin colors sharing a dip was, for the day, a radical statement about racial equality. It was true to Rogers's initial desire to choose television over the clergy—there was no rabble-rousing, no politicizing, no sermonizing. Just a simple gesture of kindness that meant so much more than what was on the surface. "Love thy neighbor as you would love thyself." Where better to exemplify that idea than in the Neighborhood?

But the progressive messages of the show weren't considered vital by all, nor was the platform through which they were delivered. In 1969, newly elected President Richard Nixon put forth policies that would have defunded PBS and other networks that wouldn't politically cooperate with his administration. Without government funding, PBS would sink into the network sewage that Fred Rogers regularly railed against. Rogers's peers and contemporaries knew that his feather-like demeanor rested on an invisible but incendiary passion for children, education, and communication, so when it came time to make a case for PBS before the Senate, Rogers was deemed the best man for the job.

For six minutes, the room was all ears. Rogers argued, in a shy but carefully modulated fashion, that PBS, along with his namesake program, was paramount to the emotional development of children in America. His program, he claimed, was not merely entertainment or "animated bombardment" but was, in fact, "an expression of care" toward each child tuning in.[183] Depicting adult men and women working out their feelings and imparting messages of self-confidence and self-love to millions of children across the nation, his episodes did far more than provide temporary stimulation—they contributed to the collective mental health of the country and the world of tomorrow.

By the end of that six minutes, the Senate had been moved to the tune of $20 million, pulling PBS from the brink of destruction with nothing but heart and soul. If you have a few moments, do browse the YouTube clip of Rogers's speech, as it's well worth the watch. It is not unlike witnessing a saint performing his most vital work.

To this day, people stand in disbelief at the majesty and crystal clarity of Rogers's soul. Rumors persist that he served time in the military, that he wore such a conservative wardrobe to cover up the tattoos he'd acquired through his time in the Navy. All of which are false. Fred Rogers was precisely as he presented himself to his audience of children and to the rest of his friends and fellow professionals. He was not a character who dropped his guard once the cameras went dark. He was a man with a message, and television was the voice of both his message and his character.

Dora the Explorer

"¡Hola!" "¡Lo hicimos!" Thirty years ago, the idea of children of all races and nationalities reciting Spanish vocabulary so casually and emphatically on television might have raised a few eyebrows, especially in a country like America, where mainstream entertainment largely catered to white Middle America throughout most, if not all, of the twentieth century. But that was one of the profound effects of *Dora the Explorer*—through its family-friendly stories and colorful characters, it created a multicultural table where everybody had a seat, where your cultural upbringing had no connection to what you could learn or enjoy.

Before the premiere of the wave-making series in 2000, creator Chris Gifford was no stranger to the wonders of television. In the early 1980s Gifford played the character Danny on *The Great Space Coaster*, a children's show created by frequent Jim Henson collaborator Kermit Love.

When Gifford became a father, he noticed that his two children, Henry and Katie, were having difficulty tackling everyday tasks. A producer for Nickelodeon by this time, he wondered if a TV series designed to teach kids how to problem-solve through fun, engaging scenarios would help his very own children.

The basic format of the series is simple but effective in engaging with its audience's creativity. Dora, the heroine of the show, is a seven-year-old Latina girl who goes on adventures, faces adversaries like the infamous fox bandit Swiper, and solves puzzles and riddles that prevent her from achieving her goals. It sounds like the familiar formula for early-childhood programming, but what distinguishes the series is its degree of interactivity, eclipsing even that of similar children's series like *Blue's Clues*. In fact, the very first episode opens not with exposition, not with a collection of wacky characters singing dream-hauntingly cheery songs, but with Dora directly asking viewers how old they are, what their names are, and how tall they are. Following the questions are pauses in which the audience is invited to insert its answers. This allows viewers to relate to Dora on a more intimate level, but also invites them to be part of the show, as if the episode and its cast of characters would be inherently incomplete without their direct participation.

As Dora journeys toward her goal, which varies from episode to episode, rather than pointing out answers to the problems presented by the story, she considers several options before asking the audience, "What do you think?" Again, she pauses for at least two or three seconds to allow the audience to reach its own conclusions. The show also doesn't punish the viewer for not getting the correct answer; it assumes that the viewer and she have conjured the same answers and implicitly encourages further participation regardless of outcome. It's a fantastic example of a series using interactivity as well as positive reinforcement to engender creative, independent thinking.

It would be the natural conclusion that a show with that kind of potential to educate and empower its viewership should reach the widest possible audience, correct? That's where the inclusivity came into play. As wrongheaded as it seems in retrospect, Dora wasn't initially named Dora at all, and she wasn't Latina. The character was originally a young girl named Nina, and it's unclear what her race or ethnicity would have been, although given the Wonder Bread nature of mainstream television pre-2000s, it's easy to guess. That's where Gifford's boss Brown Johnson—a former Nickelodeon executive who was a major force behind *Blue's Clues* and the later hit *Yo Gabba Gabba!*—worked her marketing magic. When Gifford offered the idea of introducing animal side characters to make the show more entertaining, Johnson proposed a further idea: make the main character Latina. Making the show diverse felt essential when Johnson sat down and considered how thoroughly underrepresented Latino people and culture were in mainstream media, and that what representation there was usually came in the form of comedic or passively racist stereotypes that were empowering to nobody. According to the US Census Bureau, Hispanics or Latinos made up 14 percent of the country's population in 2004,[184] but a study by the Chicano Studies Research Center at UCLA revealed that only 4 percent of regular characters on American prime-time television shows in 2004 were Latino.[185] That's a depressing statistic for any culture, let alone one as fundamentally diverse as America—considering that it was intended to be a societal melting pot, America could do better. Gifford and company saw their new series as an opportunity to create something more multicultural—by being more specific, the show's reach could be more universal.

But Chris Gifford was aware that, like many white Americans at the turn of the century, he lacked a three-dimensional understanding of Latino culture and customs. His solution: draw directly from the source. He and his cocreators, Valerie Walsh Valdes and Eric Wiener, called upon numerous consultants and educators to get the series right, creating a realistic life, background, and flavor to Dora's character and surroundings. One of those experts was Clara Rodriguez of Fordham University, a widely renowned researcher who garnered Fordham's 2003 Award for Distinguished Teaching in the Social Sciences. Among her contributions to the world of *Dora the Explorer* were selecting the kinds of music used throughout the series, creating fleshed-out and culturally accurate backstories for Dora and her family, and making these important ethnic details an organic part of the spaces Dora occupied. Though English dominated her dialogue—a predominantly English-speaking market had to be catered to—the series didn't shy away from her native

Spanish vocabulary, especially for exclamations.

Another strength of Dora is her position in the series as a strong female lead. Although she's joined later in the series by her cousin Diego, throughout the show's run, she remains an adventurous girl who solves her own problems, confronts her fears, and boldly explores new territories. In many ways, she's the perfect feminist role model for youngsters. She's not a damsel in distress, and she doesn't adhere to the aesthetic and cultural stereotypes of young female characters (hair bows, dresses, sassiness), instead presenting as earnest, brave, and equipped for outdoor activity and the kind of adventures more commonly associated with boy-centric storylines.

For the two decades it has been on the air, *Dora the Explorer* has been assisting cognitive development in young children. In a 2017 study titled "The Effects of *Dora the Explorer* on Preschool Children's Spatial Concept Acquisition and Spatial Ability," Duriye Esra Angın of Adnan Menderes University in Turkey found that children who watched the series had greater spatial intelligence, meaning the use of maps and the understanding of geography, location, and directions.[186]

The results of the experiment were undeniably in favor of the series' efficacy, and it's easy to see why: in nearly every episode of *Dora the Explorer*, the audience is invited to complete navigational puzzles. The experiment made the case that the children aren't simply watching—they're acquiring and retaining the skills needed to solve these puzzles.

Dora may not be the most palatable entertainment for parents, given that it's made for kids, but research suggests that the show benefits their children's linguistic capabilities as well as their brain and skill development. It introduces them to a set of social values that only gain importance as the children grow older, including being open to different cultures and their various customs and recognizing the capacities of young girls in proactive and mold-breaking scenarios.

So what's the conclusion here? What do all of these programs demonstrate that colloquial knowledge might not otherwise suggest? First, television is not the enemy. It never has been. Whether it's making friends through the colorful characters of *Sesame Street*, being welcomed into the nurturing ambiance of *Mister Rogers' Neighborhood*, or setting off on an adventure with *Dora the Explorer*, television has been educating and enriching children almost as long as it's been a household staple. It's been a guiding light to children across the world who might not otherwise receive the kind of encouragement more privileged families take for granted. And for all the debate about television, it seems as if we as a culture should stop taking it for granted and embrace every tool we have to prepare children for a world filled with obstacles they'll need to overcome.

Chapter 12

NETFLIX'S *13 REASONS WHY*

We've seen how storytelling can save lives, illuminate budding minds, inspire people to action, and launch careers of meaningful impact—but what about when storytelling *takes* lives?

On March 31, 2017, Netflix released all episodes of a series called *13 Reasons Why*. It depicted a young girl who takes her life after recording messages to all those in her inner circle and completing an audio diary that narrates the whole show. What was intended as an empathetic ode to the emotional struggles of adolescents led to a spike in the national suicide rate; one study found that in the nine months after the show's release, there were far more suicides in young people between the ages of ten and seventeen.[187] In addition, Google showed a 26 percent increase in searches for "how to commit suicide" in the month of the show's release.[188]

In this chapter, *13 Reasons Why* serves as a cautionary tale of what happens when storytellers don't understand the impact of their narratives, the consequences of writing something large on the big screen, and how that screen can move people to take action—or in this case, to take their own lives.

In Martin Scorsese's 1999 film *Bringing Out the Dead*, written by Paul Schrader, Frank Pierce (Nicolas Cage) is a night-shift ambulance driver in New York City. Out on a call, he and his colleague pick up a man who has just tried to commit suicide. In the kind of dark comedy we've come to expect from Schrader, Nicolas Cage's character bandages the man up, all the while explaining that if he were serious about dying, he should have cut his wrists vertically along the vein instead of horizontally—otherwise he's just wasting everyone's time.

See, up to that point in film and television, suicide was theatrical, and this character had followed suit in the monkey-see, monkey-do manner we've already read about in previous chapters from *Superman* to *The Wolf of Wall Street*. But what puts *13 Reasons Why* in a league of its own is the measure of its initial impact, the struggle to course correct, and the way in which the makers of the show still came up short in addressing the misstep.

In the series' Season 1 finale, after we've watched character Clay Jensen listen to all the tapes recorded by the deceased Hannah Baker, his former crush, describing why she took her life and how those in her inner circle were responsible for or contributed to it, Hannah draws a bath and climbs in. This is after we've seen her go to hell and back in previous episodes—losing friends; getting bullied and stalked; being lied about, slut shamed, raped, and then ignored by a counselor to whom she turns for help. In a two-minute scene, Hannah runs a razor up her forearms—vertically—and slowly bleeds out until deceased. The filmmaking is graphic and doesn't hold back, showing the cuts in close-up and lingering through what looks like a mostly painless experience as Hannah's breathing grows weak.

Criticism was immediate, with many feeling that the storytellers were romanticizing, trivializing, and even glorifying suicide. The structure of the show is such that Hannah's final act—and the way in which she delivers tapes to all those she holds responsible—is a comeuppance to those who wronged her, abused her, ignored her, or were oblivious all the while to her pain. It's as if Hannah's suicide restores a sense of justice and honor, compelling the thirteen people responsible to sit trial, hear about their wrongdoings, and face their consciences—or suffer the consequences of the tapes going public, as Hannah posthumously warns. Suicide in this way is presented as the ultimate *fuck you* to the world and those who hurt her.

Soon *13 Reasons Why* would become the most talked-about series of the year: within the first four weeks of the show's release, there were eleven million tweets about it.[189] Almost immediately, people began circulating petitions to have the show removed from the platform, emphatically asserting that suicide is not entertainment.

For the second season of the show, Netflix brought on medical and behavioral consultants in a more significant way to help mitigate the effects the storyline was having on young minds. Before episodes aired, the actors of the show made PSAs about mental health and where to find help. School boards across the country sent out notices to parents about the series' rating being TV-MA (not intended for children under seventeen) and warning about kids getting access. But with a cast of high school characters, and young people being the intended audience regardless of the rating, letters from educators could do only so much.

Two years after the release of the first season, Netflix went back and removed the controversial suicide scene from the show and announced that the series would end after Season 4. But the damage had already been done. What began as a show backed by executive producer Selena Gomez to help reach out to teens who were struggling, ultimately got the rules of impact storytelling completely wrong. Gomez herself, a singer and monumental social media icon in her own right, spoke at length in numerous interviews defending the importance of having a dialogue about such sensitive issues.

Flawed from its inception, *13 Reasons Why*'s big faux pas was the failure of Netflix and the creators to engage impact-entertainment professionals to help them better understand the potential ill effects of the narrative. Had they done their homework, they would have known that researchers at Columbia University,[190] the World Health Organization, and the American Psychological Association[191] were already quite clear on how to deal with mental health in film and television and what not to do. As noted by John W. Ayers of San Diego State University in an interview with the parenting-focused website Fatherly, "Psychiatrists have expressed grave concerns, because the show ignores the World Health Organization's validated media guidelines for preventing suicide."[192] Miguel Sabido, Albert Bandura, and all of their contemporaries in the field also could have predicted the show's harmful influence—this was as much a journey into the power of filmmaking as it was a warning of Social Impact Entertainment done wrong or at best absentmindedly.

While many said that the show mainly risked affecting younger minds more susceptible to influence, the threat by no means stopped there. Emily Bragg was nineteen when she first watched the show with her mom, Joyce Deithorn. Deithorn begged her daughter, who was bipolar, to stop viewing immediately, but Emily was too intrigued with the drama and kept watching anyway. On June 24, 2017, Emily's mom found her dead of suicide.

It's no great enigma—thoughts about suicide can lead to suicide, and that's the whole landscape lit up on the screen for four seasons. Emily's mother said in an interview with BuzzFeed News in 2019, "I truly believe that that [show] was the final thing that kind of just pushed her over the edge." In response to Netflix removing the graphic suicide scene, Deithorn said, "I guess it's them owning that they did the wrong thing," going on to say that the decision was, "way too little, too late."[193]

Those who worked on the show had varied responses to criticism. In a *Vanity Fair* op-ed in 2017, show writer Nic Sheff explained, "It seemed to me the perfect opportunity to show what an actual suicide really looks like—to dispel the myth of the quiet drifting off, and to make viewers face the reality of what happens when you jump from a burning building into something much, much worse."[194] Sheff's intent and success in his professed goal are highly debatable after watching the now-censored scene.

Helen H. Hsu, a licensed psychologist who read early drafts of the series as a consultant, told BuzzFeed News in 2017, "There does exist a very real risk of contagion for people who are very vulnerable. But there is also a much larger, gigantic community and population that really has to hear and tell stories about suicide. I've seen it save people's lives to know they're not alone as a person who suffers."[195] Of course, as Hsu implies, the intent was to help, not hurt, and surely the conversation the series kicked up did in fact reach people in need. But hundreds of people didn't have to die for us to have a global conversation about suicide and mental health. No one, not even the show's creators, would disagree about that.

A blog post on the American Psychiatric Association's website states, "The realistic portrayal of mental illness in television and movies can be an effective way to reduce stigma around psychiatric issues." That said, though, "It can be troubling if those portrayals do not show options for treatment."[196] Herein lies the problem. Never in the show was Hannah able to find help, and never was she able to get back on her feet—she simply kept getting beaten further and further into the ground. If anything, the world of the show reflects her thoughts of isolation, loneliness, and depression. It does nothing whatsoever to inspire efficacy.

Back to Miguel Sabido, the man whose serial dramas inspired millions throughout Mexico to seek out and sign up for literacy programs and implement family planning. If the goal was impact, what would *13 Reasons Why* have been with Sabido at the helm? Employing the Sabido Method, the big departure would be that after an audience was encouraged to relate to and empathize with a character, as was the case with *13 Reasons Why*, they would see her reach out and get help before committing suicide. What if Hannah sent out the tapes and escaped to a neighboring city while the drama played out, only to have her friends and family realize their mistakes? Her efficacy could then be enacted by getting understanding and assistance, having meaningful conversations, and seeking help for self-harm.

As we've clarified, efficacy is to produce in someone the desire for action leading to success. The reaching beyond the screen to say *look, she can do it, so you can, too. You can improve your life—just get out there like this person*. At Stanford in the '70s, as part of his social learning theory studies, Albert Bandura brought kids terrified of dogs into a room and showed them films of kids their age playing healthily and safely with the enemy. After only a few short viewings of these videos, when a dog was introduced into the room, the previously fearful kids would interact with only a little trepidation, since they'd seen their contemporaries forge the path.

Copycat behavior, inspiration, modeling, whatever you want to call it—when it comes to media, it's the most potent piece in creating change through impact. Storytelling 101 is to write relatable characters. What you do with those characters from then on, remember, will influence in varying degrees the trajectory of your audience. Therefore, it's the duty of all those in the craft to be informed and thoughtful about what's worked and what hasn't worked in the past. As the famous Spider-Man quote goes, "With great power comes great responsibility."

Chapter 13

THE ROAD AHEAD

Whether it's long form or episodic; radio, book, television, or movie, we have seen that across the board, Social Impact Entertainment has the power to change attitudes and beliefs. We have explored a mosaic of examples underpinning its power to influence action and even alter the course of human lives. But let us suppose that you still don't want to be a Social Impact Entertainment storyteller. There are plenty of writers and directors who have seen long and prosperous careers without so much as thinking about the power of narrative or even being conscious of the positive or negative impact of their work on audiences, outside of thrills and tears. After Frank Capra won five Academy Awards in one decade, Preston Sturges responded with a film called *Sullivan's Travels* (1941) about a blockbuster movie director throwing in his hat to make social justice pictures. In a wild series of plot points, one including mistaken identity, the film director finds himself in a chain gang among the hopeless and destitute. It is there he realizes first-hand the joy and billowing laughter entertainment itself brings to those in despair. The point being, drop the morale stories and lift people's spirits with theatrics, because that's how you are going to change the world.

The debate between Preston Sturges and Frank Capra brings to light a perceived continuum of Social Impact Entertainment, where on one end you make people laugh and on the other you deliver a message. But as Sturges showed, pure levity itself is not to be undervalued for the disenchanted and somber. Social Impact Entertainment is clearly a lot more complex and nuanced. In fact, whether it is acknowledged or not, all storytelling has impact. The question is—will storytellers be ambivalent or self-aware and clear with their intent in effecting positive impact?

If you are a storyteller reading this book, as social justice becomes more and more a part of our daily dialogue, now is your chance to lend your oxygen and give it further life. Without further speechifying, let's get started.

ENDNOTES

INTRODUCTION

1. Joan Didion, *The White Album* (New York: Farrar, Straus and Giroux, 1990), 11.
2. Martin Heidegger, "The Origin of the Work of Art," translated by Roger Berkowitz and Philippe Nonet (self-pub., Academia.edu, 2006), https://www.academia.edu/2083177/The_Origin_of_the_Work_of_Art_by_Martin_Heidegger.
3. Will Scheibel, "Rebel Masculinities of Star/Director/Text: James Dean, Nicholas Ray, and *Rebel Without a Cause*," *Journal of Gender Studies* 25, no. 2 (2016): 125–40.
4. Bill Moyers, interview of Daniel Goleman, *Bill Moyers Journal*, aired May 15, 2009, on PBS, http://www.pbs.org/moyers/journal/05152009/profile2.html.

CHAPTER 1: ENTERTAINMENT-EDUCATION OR SOCIAL IMPACT ENTERTAINMENT (SIE)

5. Arvind Singhal and Rafael Obregon, "Social Uses of Commercial Soap Operas: A Conversation with Miguel Sabido," *Journal of Development Communication* 10, no. 1 (1999): 68.
6. Arvind Singhal and Everett M. Rogers, *Entertainment-Education: A Communication Strategy for Social Change* (New York: Routledge, 2011), 49.
7. Dr. Miguel Sabido, interview by Tobias Deml and Robert Rippberger, January 11, 2018, Mexico City. Available upon request.
8. Sabido, interview.
9. Singhal and Rogers, *Entertainment-Education*, 50.
10. Miguel Sabido, "The Origins of Entertainment-Education," in *Entertainment-Education and Social Change: History, Research, and Practice*, edited by Arvind Singhal, Michael J. Cody, Everett M. Rogers, and Sabido (Mahwah, NJ: Lawrence Erlbaum, 2004), 62–63.
11. Sabido, "Origins of Entertainment-Education," 63.
12. Sabido, interview.
13. Arvind Singhal, Rafael Obregon, and Everett M. Rogers, "Reconstructing the Story of *Simplemente María*, the Most Popular Telenovela in Latin America of All Time," *International Communication Gazette* 54, no. 1 (1995): 1.
14. Singhal et al., "Reconstructing the Story," 3–4.
15. Singhal et al., "Reconstructing the Story," 10.
16. Singhal and Rogers, *Entertainment-Education*, 53.
17. Sabido, "Origins of Entertainment-Education," 64–65.
18. Sabido, interview.
19. Albert Bandura, "Social Cognitive Theory for Personal and Social Change by Enabling Media," in *Entertainment-Education and Social Change: History, Research, and Practice*, edited by Arvind Singhal, Michael J. Cody, Everett M. Rogers, and Miguel Sabido (Mahwah, NJ: Lawrence Erlbaum, 2004), 75–96.

20. Sabido, "Origins of Entertainment-Education," 68.
21. Steven J. Haggbloom et al., "The 100 Most Eminent Psychologists of the 20th Century," *Review of General Psychology* 6, no. 2 (2002): 146, https://doi.org/10.1037/1089-2680.6.2.139.
22. Robert Rippberger, host, "Albert Bandura: The Power of Soap Operas," Cinema of Change, December 13, 2017, https://www.cinemaofchange.com/albert-bandura-the-power-of-soap-operas-video/.
23. Robert Rippberger, "Albert Bandura."
24. Robert Rippberger, "Albert Bandura."
25. Robert Rippberger, "Albert Bandura."
26. Bandura "Social Cognitive Theory," 78–79.
27. Albert Bandura, Dorothea Ross, and Sheila A. Ross, "Transmission of Aggression through Imitation of Aggressive Models," *Journal of Abnormal and Social Psychology* 63, no. 3 (1961): 575–82.
28. Stephanie Hegarty, "How Soap Operas Changed the World," BBC World Service, April 27, 2012, https://www.bbc.com/news/magazine-17820571.
29. Singhal and Rogers, *Entertainment-Education*, 53.
30. Singhal and Rogers, *Entertainment-Education*, 53.
31. Singhal and Rogers, *Entertainment-Education*, 52.
32. Hegarty, "How Soap Operas Changed the World."
33. Hegarty, "How Soap Operas Changed the World."
34. Arvind Singhal and Everett M. Rogers, "*Hum Log* Story from Concept to After-Effects," in *Communication 2000 AD* (New Delhi: Indian Institute of Mass Communications, 1991), 18; Sabido, "Origins of Entertainment-Education," 64.
35. "History of Sabido Serial Dramas," Population Media Center, accessed April 24, 2020, https://www.populationmedia.org/product/sabido-history/.
36. June Carolyn Erlick, *Telenovelas in Pan-Latino Context* (New York: Routledge, 2018), 29.
37. Erlick, *Telenovelas*, 29.
38 "History of Sabido Serial Dramas," Population Media Center.
39. "History of Sabido Serial Dramas," Population Media Center.
40. Erlick, *Telenovelas*, 29.
41. Erlick, *Telenovelas*, 29.
42. Erlick, *Telenovelas*, 29.
43. Sabido, interview.
44. Sabido, interview.
45. Sabido, interview.
46. Sabido, interview.
47. Sabido, interview.

CHAPTER 2: THE STORY OF EATING DISORDERS IN FIJI

48. "Western Influences," Nakasendo Way, accessed June 20, 2020, https://www.nakasendoway.com/western-influences/.
49. Erica Goode, "Study Finds TV Alters Fiji Girls' View of Body," *New York Times*, May 20, 1999, https://www.nytimes.com/1999/05/20/world/study-finds-tv-alters-fiji-girls-view-of-body.html.

50. Corydon Ireland, "Fijian Girls Succumb to Western Dysmorphia," *Harvard Gazette*, March 19, 2009, https://news.harvard.edu/gazette/story/2009/03/fijian-girls-succumb-to-western-dysmorphia/.

CHAPTER 3: PALATABLE PUBLIC SERVICE ANNOUNCEMENTS

51. "Drunk Driving," National Highway Traffic Safety Administration, accessed June 20, 2020, https://www.nhtsa.gov/risky-driving/drunk-driving.
52. "First Drunk Driving Arrest," History.com, updated September 10, 2019, https://www.history.com/this-day-in-history/first-drunk-driving-arrest.
53. "Drunk Driving Prevention," Ad Council, accessed November 1, 2019, https://www.adcouncil.org/Our-Campaigns/The-Classics/Drunk-Driving-Prevention.
54. Alvin Powell, "Designated Driver Campaign: Harvard Center Helped to Popularize Solution to a National Problem," Harvard School of Public Health, June 1, 2010, https://www.hsph.harvard.edu/news/features/harvard-center-helped-to-popularize-solution-to-a-national-problem/.
55. "Harvard Alcohol Project," Center for Health Communication, Harvard School of Public Health, May 20, 2013, https://www.hsph.harvard.edu/chc/harvard-alcohol-project/.
56. "Poll Finds Most Americans Have Used Designated Driver Concept," Harvard School of Public Health, December 30, 1998, http://archive.sph.harvard.edu/press-releases/archives/1998-releases/press12301998.html.
57. "Harvard Alcohol Project," Center for Health Communication.
58. "Harvard Alcohol Project," Center for Health Communication.
59. "Oprah Talks to Shonda Rhimes," *O, The Oprah Magazine*, December 2006, https://www.oprah.com/omagazine/oprah-interviews-greys-anatomy-creator-shonda-rhimes/.
60. "AIDS: 25 Years Later," *Newsweek*, May 15, 2006, 27–34.
61. Kenny Malone, "The Woman behind a Secret *Grey's Anatomy* Experiment," *Only Human*, WNYC Studios, February 8, 2017, https://www.wnycstudios.org/podcasts/onlyhuman/episodes/woman-behind-greys-anatomy-hiv-pregnant.
62. Victoria Rideout, *Television as a Health Educator: A Case Study of "Grey's Anatomy"* (Menlo Park, CA: Kaiser Family Foundation, 2008), https://www.kff.org/wp-content/uploads/2013/01/7803.pdf.

CHAPTER 4: WHO NEEDS A JOB?

63. Ed Fletcher, "How Favourite TV Shows Influence Career Choices," *TheHRDIRECTOR*, February 20, 2017, https://www.thehrdirector.com/business-news/hr_in_business/favourite-tv-shows-influence-career-choices/.
64. Olivia B. Waxman, "The Real Military History behind *Top Gun*," *Time*, May 31, 2018, https://time.com/4322304/top-gun-30th-anniversary-military-history/.
65. *Top Gun*, directed by Tony Scott (1986).
66. Kirsten Acuna, "Tom Cruise's 10 Highest-Grossing Films of All Time," *Business Insider*, April 22, 2013, https://www.businessinsider.com/tom-cruises-highest-grossing-films-2013-4.
67. Mark Evje, "'Top Gun' Boosting Service Sign-Ups," *Los Angeles Times*, July 5,

1986, https://www.latimes.com/archives/la-xpm-1986-07-05-ca-20403-story.html.

68. DP/30: The Oral History of Hollywood, "DP/30: Thelma Schoonmaker Cut *The Wolf of Wall Street*," January 9, 2014, YouTube video, https://www.youtube.com/watch?v=KlKRcV4kHzg.
69. Kirsten Acuna, "Interest In Stockbroker Jobs Spiked after 'The Wolf Of Wall Street,'" *Business Insider*, March 27, 2014, https://www.businessinsider.com/interest-in-stockbroker-jobs-spiked-after-the-wolf-of-wall-street-2014-3.

CHAPTER 5: MEDIA MIMICRY: THE SIDE EFFECTS OF MODELING

70. Larry Tye, *Superman: The High-Flying History of America's Most Enduring Hero* (New York: Random House, 2012), 149.
71. Dashiell Bennett, "Why We Still Want to Believe in a Man Who Can Fly," *Atlantic*, June 14, 2013, https://www.theatlantic.com/entertainment/archive/2013/06/why-still-want-believe-man-who-can-fly/314261/.
72. "Boy Who Tried to Fly 'Like Superman' Dies," *New York Times*, February 12, 1979, https://www.nytimes.com/1979/02/12/archives/boy-who-tried-to-fly-like-superman-dies.html.
73. Erika Martinez, "'Superman' Boy Dies in Bronx Rooftop Plunge," *New York Post*, May 28, 2001, https://nypost.com/2001/05/28/superman-boy-dies-in-bronx-rooftop-plunge/.
74. Tye, *Superman*, 150.
75. *Fight Club*, directed by David Fincher (Los Angeles: 20th Century Fox, 1999).
76. Jordan Robertson, "The First Rule of Silicon Valley *Fight Club* Is . . ." NBC News, May 29, 2006, http://www.nbcnews.com/id/13037439/ns/technology_and_science-tech_and_gadgets/t/first-rule-silicon-valley-fight-club/.
77. Robertson, "The First Rule."
78. "Teen '*Fight Clubs*' Uncovered in a Texas Town," National Public Radio, August 17, 2006, https://www.npr.org/templates/story/story.php?storyId=5663318.
79. Kelli Arena and Rusty Dornin, "College Student Charged in Pipe Bomb Cases," CNN.com, May 8, 2002, http://www.cnn.com/2002/US/05/07/mailbox.pipebombs/index.html.
80. Walter Kim, "Luke Helder's Bad Trip," *Time*, May 12, 2012, http://content.time.com/time/magazine/article/0,9171,237036,00.html.
81. "Columbine Shooting," History.com, updated March 30, 2020, https://www.history.com/topics/1990s/columbine-high-school-shootings.
82. "Is *Catcher in the Rye* an Assassination Trigger?," atomicpoet (blog), January 31, 2012, https://atomicpoet.wordpress.com/2012/01/31/is-catcher-in-the-rye-an-assassination-trigger/.

CHAPTER 6: POPULATION MEDIA CENTER: BILL RYERSON

83. Charles C. Mann, "The Book That Incited a Worldwide Fear of Overpopulation," *Smithsonian Magazine*, January 2018, https://www.smithsonianmag.com/innovation/book-incited-worldwide-fear-overpopulation-180967499/.
84. Lindsey Bailey, "What Is Zero Population Growth, or ZPG?," Population

Education, May 6, 2014, https://populationeducation.org/what-zero-population-growth-or-zpg/.
85. "Maternal Mortality: Key Facts," World Health Organization, September 19, 2019, https://www.who.int/en/news-room/fact-sheets/detail/maternal-mortality.
86. "About Us," Population Media Center, accessed April 2, 2020, https://www.populationmedia.org/about-us/.
87. MTV Latin America, "MTV Latin America, Population Media Center and the United Nations Population Fund Launch Multiplatform Campaign SexySex to Empower Young People on Sexual Health and Violence Prevention," PR Newswire, December 3, 2012, https://www.prnewswire.com/news-releases/mtv-latin-america-population-media-center-and-the-united-nations-population-fund-launch-multiplatform-campaign-sexysex-to-empower-young-people-on-sexual-health-and-violence-prevention-181854211.html.
88. "About Teen Pregnancy," Centers for Disease Control and Prevention, March 1, 2019, https://www.cdc.gov/teenpregnancy/about/index.htm.
89. "Helen Wang," Faculty Spotlight, Department of Communication, University at Buffalo, December 7, 2018, http://www.buffalo.edu/cas/communication/research/faculty-spotlight.host.html/content/shared/cas/communication/module-content/faculty-spotlight/faculty_wang.detail.html.
90. Maanvi Singh, "'East Los High' Isn't Just a Soapy Teen Drama—It's Also a Science Experiment," *Code Switch*, National Public Radio, January 11, 2016, https://www.npr.org/sections/codeswitch/2016/01/11/451940463/east-los-high-isnt-just-a-soapy-teen-drama-its-also-a-science-experiment.
91. "*East Los High*," Population Media Center, accessed April 2, 2020, https://www.populationmedia.org/projects/east-los-high/.
92. "SexySex (*Ultimo Año*)," The HIV/AIDS Network, The Communication Initiative, February 11, 2013, http://www.comminit.com/hiv-aids/content/sexysex-ultimo-año.
93. John F. May, "Niger Has the World's Highest Birth Rate—and That May Be a Recipe for Unrest," The Conversation US, March 21, 2019, https://theconversation.com/niger-has-the-worlds-highest-birth-rate-and-that-may-be-a-recipe-for-unrest-108654.
94. "Total Fertility Rate 2020," World Population Review, February 17, 2020, http://worldpopulationreview.com/countries/total-fertility-rate/.
95. "Niger Population 2020," World Population Review, February 17, 2020, http://worldpopulationreview.com/countries/niger-population/.
96. Kriss Barker, "*Gobe da Haske* (Tomorrow Will Be a Brighter Day)," The Entertainment-Education Network—Africa, The Communication Initiative, March 21, 2011, http://www.comminit.com/edutain-africa/content/gobe-da-haske-tomorrow-will-be-brighter-day.
97. "*Gobe da Haske*," Population Media Center, accessed August 6, 2019, https://www.populationmedia.org/projects/gobe-da-haske/.
98. *Population Media Center 2007 Annual Report* (Shelburne, VT: Population Media Center, July 31, 2008), 12, https://www.populationmedia.org/wp-content/uploads/2008/08/pmc_ar_2007.pdf.
99. "World Population History/World Population Projections," World

Population Review, accessed April 8, 2020, https://worldpopulationreview.com/#worldPopHistory.

CHAPTER 7: WILL & GRACE: HOMOSEXUALITY IN THE AMERICAN LIVING ROOM

100. "TV Winners & Losers: Numbers Racket: A Final Tally of the Season's Shows," *Entertainment Weekly*, June 4, 1999, https://web.archive.org/web/20080213010636/http://www.geocities.com/Hollywood/4616/ew0604.html.

101. Marriage Equality," *Huffington Post*, May 6, 2012, https://www.huffpost.com/entry/vice-president-biden-gay-marriage_n_1489235?guccounter=1.

CHAPTER 8: EARLY AUTEURS: THE GOOD, THE BAD, AND THE UGLY

102. "Top Movie Moments; #8: 'Frankly, My Dear, I Don't Give a Damn,'" IGN, accessed August 6, 2019, https://www.ign.com/top/movie-moments/8.

103. Gerald Clarke, *Capote: A Biography* (New York: Simon & Schuster, 1988; Rosetta Books, 2013), https://books.google.com/books?id=nUqqAAAAQBAJ.

104. Colin Jacobson, review of *Breakfast at Tiffany's: The Centennial Collection*, DVD Movie Guide, January 13, 2009, http://www.dvdmg.com/breakfastattiffanyscc.shtml.

105. Stephen Magagnini, "Mickey Rooney Upset at Racism Allegations," *Deseret News*, September 7, 2008, https://www.deseretnews.com/article/700256494/Mickey-Rooney-upset-at-racism-allegations.html.

106. Magagnini, "Mickey Rooney Upset."

107. David Pilgrim, "Interracial Marriages - 2006 - Question of the Month - Jim Crow Museum," Ferris.edu, February 2006, https://www.ferris.edu/HTMLS/news/jimcrow/question/2006/february.htm.

108. "Loving v. Virginia," History.com, November 17, 2017, https://www.history.com/topics/civil-rights-movement/loving-v-virginia.

109. Karen Thomas, "Bernie Will Be Spencer in New 'Coming to Dinner,'" *USA Today*, July 11, 2003.

110. Martin Luther King Jr., "The American Dream" (speech, Drew University, Madison, NJ, February 5, 1964), https://depts.drew.edu/lib/archives/online_exhibits/king/speech/theamericandream.pdf.

111. Lou Lumenick, "Why 'Birth of a Nation' Is Still the Most Racist Movie Ever," *New York Post*, February 7, 2015, https://nypost.com/2015/02/07/why-birth-of-a-nation-is-still-the-most-controversial-movie-ever/.

112. Godfrey Cheshire, "Why No One Is Celebrating the 100th Anniversary of the Feature Film," *Vulture*, February 6, 2015, https://www.vulture.com/2015/02/why-we-arent-celebrating-100-years-of-movies.html.

113. "D. W. Griffith's *The Birth of a Nation*," The Rise and Fall of Jim Crow, THIRTEEN, 2002, https://www.thirteen.org/wnet/jimcrow/stories_events_birth.html.

114. Mark E. Benbow, "Birth of a Quotation: Woodrow Wilson and 'Like Writing History with Lightning,'" *Journal of the Gilded Age and Progressive Era* 9, no. 4 (2010): 509–33, www.jstor.org/stable/20799409.

115. Alexis Clark, "How 'The Birth of a Nation' Revived the Ku Klux Klan," History.com, updated July 29, 2019, https://www.history.com/news/kkk-birth-of-a-nation-film.
116. Richard Corliss, "D. W. Griffith's *The Birth of a Nation* 100 Years Later: Still Great, Still Shameful," *Time*, March 3, 2015, https://time.com/3729807/d-w-griffiths-the-birth-of-a-nation-10/.
117. Saul McLeod, "Bandura—Social Learning Theory," Simply Psychology, February 5, 2016. https://www.simplypsychology.org/bandura.html.
118. Roger Ebert, "*A Clockwork Orange*," RogerEbert.com, February 2, 1972, https://www.rogerebert.com/reviews/a-clockwork-orange-1972.
119. Devin Faraci, "Why Stanley Kubrick Banned *A Clockwork Orange*," Birth.Movies.Death., August 1, 2013, https://birthmoviesdeath.com/2013/08/01/the-disappearance-of-a-clockwork-orange.
120. "Culture Shock: Flashpoints: Theater, Film, and Video: Stanley Kubrick's *A Clockwork Orange*," PBS, 2000, https://www.pbs.org/wgbh/cultureshock/flashpoints/theater/clockworkorange.html.
121. Peter Bradshaw, "The Old Ultra-Violence," Guardian (London), March 3, 2000, https://www.theguardian.com/film/2000/mar/03/fiction.
122. Frank Capra, *The Name above the Title: An Autobiography* (New York: Macmillan, 1971), 6–7.
123. Frank Capra, *Frank Capra: Interviews*, ed. Leland Poague (Jackson: University Press of Mississippi, 2004), xxii.
124. "It Happened One Night," *Variety*, February 26, 1934, https://variety.com/1934/film/reviews/it-happened-one-night-2-1200410931/.
125. "Frank Capra: Quotes," IMDb.com, accessed December 27, 2019, https://m.imdb.com/name/nm0001008/quotes.
126. "*Mr. Deeds Goes to Town* (1936)," The Numbers, accessed June 21, 2020, https://www.the-numbers.com/movie/Mr-Deeds-Goes-To-Town.
127. Frank S. Nugent, "Columbia's Film of Hilton's 'Lost Horizon' Opens at the Globe—'Maid of Salem' at the Paramount," *New York Times*, March 4, 1937, https://www.nytimes.com/1937/03/04/archives/the-screen-columbias-film-of-hiltons-lost-horizon-opens-at-the.html.
128. Joseph McBride, *Frank Capra: The Catastrophe of Success* (Jackson: University Press of Mississippi, 1992), 366.
129. Frank Capra, *The Name above the Title: An Autobiography* (New York: Macmillan, 1971), 383.
130. Jeanin Basinger, Frances Goodrich, Leonard Maltin, and the Trustees of the Frank Capra Archives, *The "It's a Wonderful Life" Book* (New York; Alfred A. Knopf, 1986), 85.

CHAPTER 9: MEGA-IMPACT AND MEGA-BLOCKBUSTERS

131. "Video: Roger Ebert on Empathy," RogerEbert.com, April 4, 2018, https://www.rogerebert.com/empathy/video-roger-ebert-on-empathy.
132. "Top Lifetime Grosses," Box Office Mojo, accessed April 14, 2020, https://www.boxofficemojo.com/alltime/world/.
133. Nick Evans, "*Avatar*'s Box Office Record Is Even More Impressive after

Avengers: Endgame," CinemaBlend, June 4, 2019, https://www.cinemablend.com/news/2474332/avatars-box-office-record-is-even-more-impressive-after-avengers-endgame.

134. Todd McCarthy, "Review: 'The Social Network,'" IndieWire, September 20, 2010, https://www.indiewire.com/2010/09/review-the-social-network-228005/.

135. Mike Ryan, "Q&A: James Cameron Talks about *Avatar*'s Re-release," *Vanity Fair*, August 27, 2010, https://www.vanityfair.com/hollywood/2010/08/qa-james-cameron-talks-about-avatars-re-release.

136. "*Avatar*," Rotten Tomatoes, accessed April 14, 2020, https://www.rottentomatoes.com/m/avatar.

137. Roger Ebert, "Cameron Retains His Crown," RogerEbert.com, December 11, 2009, https://www.rogerebert.com/reviews/avatar-2009.

138. Armond White, "Blue in the Face: James Cameron Delivers Dumb Escapism with His Expensive Special Effects in 'Avatar,'" *New York Press*, December 15, 2009.

139. Jessica Lee, "'Avatar' Activism: James Cameron Joins Indigenous Struggles Worldwide," *Indypendent*, April 26, 2010, https://indypendent.org/2010/04/avatar-activism-james-cameron-joins-indigenous-struggles-worldwide/.

140. Eric Ditzian, "James Cameron Says 'Avatar' Is Inspiring Environmental Activism," MTV News, February 17, 2010, http://www.mtv.com/news/1632038/james-cameron-says-avatar-is-inspiring-environmental-activism/.

141. *Titanic*, limited 3D ed., Blu-ray, directed by James Cameron (Hollywood, CA: Paramount Home Entertainment, 2012).

142. Sarah Marshall, "The Incredible True Story of How 'Titanic' Got Made," BuzzFeed News, December 17, 2017, https://www.buzzfeednews.com/article/sarahmarshall/20-years-ago-titanic-took-over-the-world-heres-why.

143. James Cameron, *Titanic* screenplay, Internet Movie Script Database (IMSDb), accessed April 16, 2020, https://www.imsdb.com/scripts/Titanic.html.

144. "I am the master of my fate, / I am the captain of my soul."

145. "All Time Worldwide Box Office," The Numbers, accessed June 21, 2020, https://www.the-numbers.com/box-office-records/worldwide/all-movies/cumulative/all-time.

145. *The Making of* Star Wars, directed by Robert Guenette (Los Angeles: 20th Century Fox Television, 1977).

147. *Star Wars: Episode IV—A New Hope*, directed by George Lucas (1977).

148. *Joseph Campbell and the Power of Myth*, episode 1, "The Hero's Adventure," aired June 21, 1988, on PBS.

149. "*Star Wars Ep. I—The Phantom Menace* (1999)," The Numbers, accessed April 17, 2020, https://www.the-numbers.com/movie/Star-Wars-Ep-I-The-Phantom-Menace#tab=summary.

150. Mark Kermode, "Mark Kermode Reviews *Star Trek: Into Darkness*," Kermode and Mayo's Film Review, May 10, 2013, YouTube video, https://www.youtube.com/watch?v=nituwJflRaU.

151. Spill.com, "*Star Trek: Into Darkness*—Spill Audio Review," May 17, 2013, https://www.youtube.com/watch?v=TwwafXtspoE.

152. Scott Dadich, "Lucky VII," *Wired*, November 2015, https://www.wired.com/2015/11/star-wars-force-awakens-jj-abrams-interview/.

153. "J J Abrams Discusses *Star Wars The Force Awakens* Aol BUILD Interview," Love Star Wars, December 4, 2015, YouTube video, https://www.youtube.com/watch?v=5bE7zSyjNSs.
154. "Star Wars Is a Game-Changer, Awakening the Feminist Force in Little Girls Everywhere," *Guardian* (London), December 29, 2015, https://www.theguardian.com/commentisfree/2015/dec/30/star-wars-is-a-game-changer-awakening-the-feminist-force-in-little-girls-everywhere.
155. Charlie Spiering, "Disney: 'Strong, Empowered' Females in *Star Wars* Is 'Purposeful,'" *Breitbart*, April 7, 2016, https://www.breitbart.com/politics/2016/04/07/disney-strong-empowered-female-star-wars-purposeful/.
156. Spiering, "Disney."
157. David G. Brown, "Why *Star Wars: The Force Awakens* Is a Social Justice Propaganda Film," *Return of Kings* (blog), December 20, 2015, https://www.returnofkings.com/75991/why-star-wars-the-force-awakens-is-a-social-justice-propaganda-film.
158. Ruth Umoh, "How the Man behind Marvel's 'Avengers' Went from Washing Cars to a $1 Billion Blockbuster," CNBC.com, May 7, 2018, https://www.cnbc.com/2018/05/04/marvel-president-kevin-feige-went-from-washing-cars-to-the-avengers.html.
159. Matt Singer, "Dark Universe, a Shared Universe for Universal Monsters, Dies at 1," ScreenCrush, January 28, 2019, https://screencrush.com/rip-dark-universe/.
160. Frank Pallotta, "'Avengers: Endgame' Passes 'Avatar' to Become the Highest-Grossing Film Ever," CNN, July 21, 2019, https://www.cnn.com/2019/07/20/media/avengers-endgame-avatar-box-office/index.html.
161. Mary Magoulick, "What Is Myth?" *Folklore Connections* (blog), revised 2015, accessed April 17, 2020, https://faculty.gcsu.edu/custom-website/mary-magoulick/defmyth.htm.
162. Heidi MacDonald, "In a World of Too Many Cons, San Diego Is Still King," *Publishers Weekly*, July 6, 2018, https://www.publishersweekly.com/pw/by-topic/industry-news/comics/article/77455-in-a-world-of-too-many-cons-san-diego-is-still-king.html.
163. Harriet Sherwood, "'Christianity as Default Is Gone': The Rise of a Non-Christian Europe," *Guardian* (London), March 20, 2018, https://www.theguardian.com/world/2018/mar/21/christianity-non-christian-europe-young-people-survey-religion.
164. Neil Monahan and Saeed Ahmed, "There Are Now as Many Americans Who Claim No Religion as There Are Evangelicals and Catholics, a Survey Finds," CNN, updated April 26, 2019, https://www.cnn.com/2019/04/13/us/no-religion-largest-group-first-time-usa-trnd/index.html.
165. Allen Downey, "The U.S. Is Retreating from Religion," Scientific American Blog Network, October 20, 2017, https://blogs.scientificamerican.com/observations/the-u-s-is-retreating-from-religion/.
166. "Producers Say No to *Jurassic Park 4*," ComingSoon.net, December 8, 2008, https://www.comingsoon.net/movies/news/51101-producers-say-no-to-jurassic-park-4.
167. "*Jurassic World*: Steven Spielberg & Colin Trevorrow Behind the Scenes Movie

Interview," ScreenSlam, May 31, 2015, YouTube video, https://www.youtube.com/watch?v=PFDI0KcnRFA.

168. Peter Sciretta, "Extensive *Jurassic World* Interview with Director Colin Trevorrow," */Film* (blog), April 30, 2015, https://www.slashfilm.com/colin-trevorrow-jurassic-world-interview.

169. "*Jurassic World* and Its Resemblance to *Blackfish*," *Blackfish* website, June 17, 2015, http://www.blackfishmovie.com/news/2015/9/21/mc4blzo30poa8d088puc1yt2uad511.

170. Roberto A. Ferdman, "Chart: What the Documentary 'Blackfish' Has Done to SeaWorld," *Washington Post*, December 12, 2014, https://www.washingtonpost.com/news/wonk/wp/2014/12/12/chart-what-the-documentary-blackfish-has-done-to-seaworld/.

171. "*The Lost World: Jurassic Park*," Box Office Mojo, accessed August 6, 2019, https://www.boxofficemojo.com/movies/?id=jurassicpark2.htm.

172. "*Jurassic Park III*," Box Office Mojo, accessed April 19, 2020, https://www.boxofficemojo.com/movies/?id=jurassicpark3.htm.

173. See, for instance, Emily Yahr, "Does 'Jurassic World' Remind You of 'Blackfish'? How a Dinosaur Movie Tackled Animal Rights," *Washington Post*, June 15, 2015, https://www.washingtonpost.com/news/arts-and-entertainment/wp/2015/06/15/does-jurassic-world-remind-you-of-blackfish-how-a-dinosaur-movie-tackled-animal-rights/; and Caitlin Jill Anders, "*Jurassic World* Is Eerily Like Seaworld, and Everyone Noticed," The Dodo, June 15, 2015, https://www.thedodo.com/jurassic-world-similarities-to-seaworld-tweets-1202373428.html.

174. "Watch: John Hargrove Takes Down SeaWorld on *The Daily Show*, SeaWorld's #AskSeaWorld Campaign Backfires Spectacularly," PETA, March 27, 2015, https://www.peta.org/blog/watch-john-hargrove-takes-down-seaworld-on-the-daily-show-seaworlds-askseaworld-campaign-backfires/.

175. Molly Lunch, "SeaWorld tried to answer questions on Twitter, and it did not go well," Mashable, March 27, 2015, https://mashable.com/2015/03/27/seaworld-twitter-questions/.

176. Anders, "*Jurassic World*."

177. Josh Kosman, "SeaWorld Stock Sinks 50% in 2014," *New York Post*, November 16, 2014, https://nypost.com/2014/11/16/seaworld-stock-sinks-50-in-2014/.

178. Amber Jamieson, "SeaWorld Decides to Stop Killer Whale Breeding Program," *Guardian* (New York), March 17, 2016, https://www.theguardian.com/us-news/2016/mar/17/seaworld-to-stop-breeding-killer-whales-orcas-blackfish.

179. Paula Landry and Stephen R. Greenwald, *The Business of Film: A Practical Introduction*, 2nd ed. (New York: Routledge, 2018), chap. 7, https://www.google.com/books/edition/The_Business_of_Film/_WJgDwAAQBAJ.

CHAPTER 10: DAVID AND GOLIATH

180. Jason Silverstein, "There Were More Mass Shootings than Days in 2019," CBS News, updated January 2, 2020, https://www.cbsnews.com/news/mass-shootings-2019-more-mass-shootings-than-days-so-far-this-year/.

181. "Pelman v. McDonald's Corp.," 237 F. Supp. 2d 512 (S.D.N.Y. 2003), https://law.

justia.com/cases/federal/district-courts/FSupp2/237/512/2462869/.

182. Maddie Caso, "The 'Super' Side Effects of Fast Food," ENTITY, February 9, 2017, https://www.entitymag.com/effects-fast-food-told-by-morgan-spurlock-super-size-me/.
183. Tatiana Morales, "From 2004: 'Super Size Me,'" CBS News, May 6, 2004, https://www.cbsnews.com/news/from-2004-super-size-me/.
184. Errol Morris, "The Ashtray: This Contest of Interpretation (Part 5)," *New York Times*, March 10, 2011, https://opinionator.blogs.nytimes.com/2011/03/10/the-ashtray-this-contest-of-interpretation-part-5/.
185. Amanda Meyncke, "Interview: Errol Moris on *Tabloid*," MTV News, July 15, 2011, http://www.mtv.com/news/2766605/interview-errol-morris-on-tabloid/.
186. Ron Rosenbaum, "Errol Morris: The Thinking Man's Detective," *Smithsonian*, March 2012, https://www.smithsonianmag.com/arts-culture/errol-morris-the-thinking-mans-detective-99424163/.
187. Laura Bell, "Groups Expel Texas Psychiatrist Known for Murder Cases," *Dallas Morning News*, July 26, 1995, https://web.archive.org/web/20090307034749/http://ccadp.org/DrDeath.htm.

CHAPTER 11:
STORYTELLING AND EDUCATION

188. US Department of Education, *A Matter of Equity: Preschool in America* (April 2015), 3, https://www2.ed.gov/documents/early-learning/matter-equity-preschool-america.pdf.
189. Richard T. Murphy, "Educational Effectiveness of *Sesame Street*: A Review of the First Twenty Years of Research 1969–1989," *ETS Research Report Series* 1991, no. 2 (1991), https://doi.org/10.1002/j.2333-8504.1991.tb01422.x.
190. Murphy, "Educational Effectiveness," 20–21.
191. Murphy, "Educational Effectiveness," 21.
192. Murphy, "Educational Effectiveness," 22.
193. Murphy, "Educational Effectiveness," 27.
194. The lyrics to the *Mister Rogers' Neighborhood* theme song, "Won't You Be My Neighbor," can be found on the official website of the show at https://www.misterrogers.org/the-music/.
195. Jon Webb, "Webb: It's 50 Years since 'Mister Rogers' Debut. Here He Is Explaining Violence to Children," *Courier & Press* (Evansville, IN), February 19, 2018, https://www.courierpress.com/story/opinion/columnists/jon-webb/2018/02/19/webb-its-50-years-since-mister-rogers-debut-heres-him-explaining-violence-kids/352099002/.
196. Chris Azzopardi, "Mister Rogers's Gay, Black Friend François Clemmons Wears Tiaras Now," *Vanity Fair*, June 27, 2018, https://www.vanityfair.com/hollywood/2018/06/mister-rogers-neighborhood-wont-you-be-my-neighbor-francois-clemmons-officer-clemmons-fred-rogers.
197. Azzopardi, "Mister Rogers's."
198. "May 1, 1969: Fred Rogers Testifies before the Senate Subcommittee on Communications," Danieldeibler, February 8, 2015, YouTube video, 6:50, https://www.youtube.com/watch?v=fKy7ljRr0AA.

199. US Census Bureau, "The American Community—Hispanics: 2004," February 2007, https://www.census.gov/library/publications/2007/acs/acs-03.html.
200. Alison R. Hoffman and Chon A. Noriega, *Looking for Latino Regulars on Prime-Time Television: The Fall 2004 Season* (Los Angeles: UCLA Chicano Studies Research Center, 2004), 2, http://www.chicano.ucla.edu/files/crr_04Dec2004_000.pdf.
201. Duriye Esra Angin, "The Effects of *Dora the Explorer* on Preschool Children's Spatial Concept Acquisition and Spatial Ability," *European Scientific Journal* 13, no. 1 (2017): 39–53, http://eujournal.org/index.php/esj/article/view/8739.

CHAPTER 12: NETFLIX'S 13 REASONS WHY

202. "'13 Reasons Why' and Media Effects on Suicide," Penn Today, November 20, 2019, https://penntoday.upenn.edu/news/13-reasons-why-and-media-effects-suicide.
203. Brandon Katz, "Netflix's '13 Reasons Why' Linked to Increase in Suicide," *Observer* (New York), February 8, 2018, https://observer.com/2018/02/netflixs-13-reasons-why-linked-suicide-increase/.
204. Elizabeth Wagmeister, "Netflix's '13 Reasons Why' Is Most Tweeted About Show of 2017," *Variety*, April 21, 2017, https://variety.com/2017/tv/news/netflix-13-reasons-why-twitter-most-popular-show-2017-1202392460/.
205. Madelyn Gould, Pablo Goldberg, and Mirjana Domakonda, "New Show *13 Reasons Why* Reinforces Dangerous Teen Suicide Myths," Medscape, June 15, 2017, https://childadolescentpsych.cumc.columbia.edu/articles/new-show-13-reasons-why-reinforces-dangerous-teen-suicide-myths.
206. Jennifer B. Dwyer, Swathi Krishna, and Chandan Khandai, "13 Mental Health Questions about '13 Reasons Why,'" APA Blogs, American Psychiatric Association, April 18, 2017, https://www.psychiatry.org/news-room/apa-blogs/apa-blog/2017/04/13-mental-health-questions-about-13-reasons-why.
207. Lauren Vinopal, "Netflix's '13 Reasons Why' May Cause a Suicide Spike, Scientists Caution," Fatherly, July 31, 2017, https://www.fatherly.com/health-science/psychology/netflix-13-reasons-why-suicidal-thoughts/.
208. Krystie Lee Yandoli, "The Suicide Edit in '13 Reasons Why' Is 'Too Little, Too Late' for This Mom Whose Daughter Killed Herself," BuzzFeed News, July 17, 2019, https://www.buzzfeednews.com/article/krystieyandoli/13-reasons-why-suicide-mom-daughter-netflix-cut-scene.
209. Nic Sheff, "*13 Reasons Why* Writer: Why We Didn't Shy Away from Hannah's Suicide," *Vanity Fair*, April 19, 2017, https://www.vanityfair.com/hollywood/2017/04/13-reasons-why-suicide-controversy-nic-sheff-writer.
210. Yandoli, "Suicide Edit."
211. Dwyer et al., "13 Mental Health Questions."

www.ingramcontent.com/pod-product-compliance
Lightning Source LLC
Chambersburg PA
CBHW060316030426
42336CB00011B/1080
9781587906015